GROWING IN HOLINESS

The Hebrew Calendar Day by Day

A  Book ©

S. Creeger, BAJS, MTh.

This booklet is a BEKY Book publication:
Books Encouraging the Kingdom of Yeshua.
www.bekybooks.com

Cover design by Rubel Photography, Mt. Juliet, TN
Artwork by LeAnn Hoffman

Special thanks to the following: Hollisa Alewine, Rhea Rohr, Yitzak Waxman and Juliane Jackson. This book is a reality, because you cared enough to pray, encourage, edit, and type.

DEDICATION

Yeshuel Ohev, you have brought joy and blessing into our lives.

You are indeed beloved.

CONTENTS

GLOSSARY

Adonai - Our Lord.

Brit Chadasha - New Testament; literally "Renewed Covenant."

Challah - A special bread made for Shabbat and some Jewish holidays. It is generally braided and a small piece set aside as an offering from the main loaves prior to baking.

Erev Shabbat - Literally, "Evening Shabbat," beginning Friday evening at sunset.

G-d - God, written this way to respect the names we use for God to help develop our sensitivity not to casually refer to God.

Haftorah - Literally "taking leave," or "dismissing." It is a selection of Scripture from the Prophets. It can also be spelled Haftarah.

HaShem - Literally, "The Name," used by Orthodox Jews instead of "God" or "Lord" out of respect for the holiness of God's name.

Havdalah - literally "separation/distinction" ritual that acknowledges the close of Shabbat and the beginning of the work week.

Kashrut - The body of Jewish law that defines what foods can be eaten or not and how those foods must be prepared.

Ketubah - The Jewish marriage contract, similar to a prenuptial agreement, citing the groom's responsibilities to his wife. It makes provision for the wife and her dependents in the event of his death or divorce.

Kiddush - Literally, "sanctification." It is the blessing recited over a cup of wine or grape juice when ushering in the Sabbath on Friday evening or at other Jewish holidays.

L-rd - Lord, written this way to respect the names we use for God to help develop sensitivity not to casually refer to God.

Moedim - The seven festivals instructed in the Scriptures, such as Passover (Pesach), Pentecost (Shavuot, Weeks), or Tabernacles (Sukkot).

Parsha - Literally, "portion." A selected Biblical reading from the Torah for the weekly Shabbat. The plural is parshiyot.

Ruach HaKodesh - The Holy Spirit.

Seder - Literally, "order." Seder is the religious ritual service which includes dinner the first and possibly second night of Passover.

Shabbat - The Hebrew word for Sabbath. The plural is Shabbatot.

Shehecheyanu - Literally, "Who has given us life." A prayer of thanksgiving said when we experience something new, or to celebrate special occasions. If HaShem had not granted us life, we would not be here to experience the occasion.

Shofar - The horn of a kosher animal, i.e., a ram or gazelle horn that has been hollowed out so that it can be blown.

Ta'anit - A fast.

Talmidim - Hebrew word for "disciples."

Torah - The first five books of the Bible, called the Pentateuch in Greek.

Teshuvah - Literally, "return." The word is used to express the concept of repentance in Judaism – in essence returning to G-d and His ways.

Tzom - A fast.

INTRODUCTION

For many who enjoy reading the Bible, there are often parts that present a puzzle, particularly when modern observance seems different from what appears in the Scriptures. For many Christians, the Old Testament (*Tanakh*) is a particular challenge. On the other hand, the New Testament (*Brit Chadasha*) contains the same holidays, Sabbath, customs, fasts, and other details of the Tanakh. Having a dictionary of those observances is vital to understanding the Tanakh, the foundation to which Yeshua (Jesus), the disciples, and the apostles referenced in 80%-85% of the Newer Testament.

Such a "dictionary" could be extensive, yet to someone who does not have time to attend a seminary or Bible school, where to start? The Jewish calendar is a great place to start learning the foundational set times appointed by the Father in Heaven, for He set these times from the creation of the earth. Jewish calendars ensure that Israel continues to observe these foundational principles of holiness and blessing from generation to generation.

To grow in His Word is to grow in holiness day by day. In His infinite wisdom, G-d provided His children daily, monthly, seasonal, and annual instructions on how to increase in holiness by respecting His set times for growth. There are even opportunities for experiencing growth by knowing the cycles of seven years and fifty-year jubilees. Engaging these appointed times has the added benefit of making one wise in the prophetic implications of each word of Scripture, for there are no idle words between Genesis and Revelation. All is G-d-breathed and beneficial to disciples of Yeshua.

The best use of this booklet is to have a traditional

Jewish calendar handy for reference and to turn to the glossary frequently for explanations of new words.

1

SHABBAT שַׁבָּת

On the first day of Creation, HaShem (G-d) separated evening from morning, and then He declared that measure of time to be a day. He created the world in six days (naming and numbering them one through six), and on the seventh day, Shabbat (שַׁבָּת), He rested. He thereby set aside a special day, giving it not a numerical value (seven) but a name, Shabbat (שבת). In Hebrew, Shabbat means to cease and to stop. Mankind is to stop all work and cease to create anything, emulating our Creator who had finished all of His work and rested. The Erev Shabbat [1] prayer is:

> Blessed are You, Adonai Eloheinu [2], King of the universe, who sanctifies us with His commandments and has given us as an inheritance His Holy Sabbath in love and in favor, a reminder of the works of creation. For it is the first day among the festivals of holiness, a remembrance of the Exodus from Egypt. For You have chosen us from amongst all peoples and have given us as an inheritance, Your Sabbath, in love and favor. Blessed are You, Adonai, who makes the Sabbath holy.

Shabbat is an inheritance for us and our children. It is a gift given in love and in favor, not a day of limitations and restrictions. Even before there was a nation called Israel or the Jewish people, Shabbat is a day set apart to help mankind become a holy creation. It is the *first* day among the festivals of holiness. Throughout the centuries it has been said, "As much as the Jew has kept Shabbat, so has the Shabbat kept the Jew."

All come to the Shabbat table having bathed and wearing good clothes to welcome in the Shabbat. Traditionally, those who desire to observe Shabbat light two candles[3], reminding each family of the commandments to remember (*zachor*) and keep (*shamor*) the Sabbath day holy (Exodus 20:8). Isaiah 58:13 clarifies that Israel is to honor (*kavod*) and delight (*oneg*) in Shabbat observance. The Torah prohibits kindling a fire on Shabbat, so candles are lit

1. Erev Shabbat is Sabbath evening. It begins Friday night at sunset.

2. L-rd, our G-d

3. Traditionally candles are lit 18 minutes prior to sunset.

12

before sundown.

The rabbis knew that Jews would find their homes in darkness on Erev Shabbat, and so the practice of lighting candles for Shabbat was introduced. This allowed families to more fully enjoy the Shabbat meal; they could see the food and each other! Although it is not a Torah commandment, it is easy to see the practicality of the rabbis' decision to have households light candles for Shabbat.

Some individuals light only one, others may light more. Some families add an additional candle for each member of the household. As soon as one's daughter is old enough to say the blessings, she may begin to kindle her own Shabbat candle. Women are given the privilege and honor to light the Shabbat candles, although men may light them as well.

It is customary to place some coins in the tzedekah[4] box prior to lighting the candles. Generally, once the box is full, the money is given either to a charitable organization or a person in need. It is a wonderful way to teach children about caring for those less fortunate and to remind ourselves of the need to do so.

A blessing follows the lighting of the candles.

> Blessed are You, Adonai Eloheinu,
> King of the universe, Who sanctifies
> us with His commandments, and
> commands us to light the Sabbath
> candles.

The person leading Kiddush[5] may have a special, decorated cup for the wine blessing.   A cup of wine or grape juice is poured for each person, and everyone says the Kiddush together:

> Blessed are You, Adonai Eloheinu,
> King of the universe, Creator of the

4. Tzedekah – literally justice (charity)

5. Kiddush- sanctification

13

fruit of the vine."

A loaf or two of *challah*[6] bread has been baked for Shabbat[7], and a decorative cover is placed atop it. Everyone says the blessing for the challah together:

> Blessed are You, Adonai Eloheinu,
> King of the universe, who brings forth
> bread from the earth.

Being together as a family around the Shabbat table provides a wonderful opportunity to bless one's spouse and children. Families sing songs, pray psalms, discuss the Torah portion, and delight in His rest.

Lighting the candles, drinking the wine, and eating the challah causes Israel as a people to acknowledge the holiness of the time of Shabbat. This ritual practice has created a spatial sanctification around families and homes. Shabbat speech is not about the mundane trials of the workday; speech, thoughts, and actions are elevated to reflect the connection one has with the Creator. Likewise, worshipers are spiritually elevated as they enter in to this holy time.

6. Challah-braided bread especially baked for Shabbat

On Shabbat, families do not work, but instead mankind is gifted the "day off" by the Creator to rest with Him. After synagogue service, many will play with their children, read spiritually uplifting books, study Torah, visit with friends, or enjoy a nap.

7. For a challah recipe, see Appendix A

Each Shabbat has a Torah portion (Parsha). פרשה

8 . For more information on the structure of the Biblical calendar, see K. Gallagher's BEKY Book, *The Biblical New Moon: A Beginner's Guide for Celebrating.*

The entire Torah (Genesis to Deuteronomy) is read each year. The rabbis long ago established the reading order. In years that are not leap years (on the Jewish calendar)[8], some Torah portions may be doubled in order that all of the Scripture is read for that year. Each *parsha* has a Hebrew name which does not necessarily indicate the topic, but is

14

generally one of the first words that start that portion, e.g., *Ki Tisa* (Exodus 30:12 - "when you take"). See Appendix B for a complete list.

Each Shabbat has a Haftorah הפטרה portion.

A *Haftorah* portion is a reading from the Prophets. Haftorah means "parting," or "taking leave." The rabbis assigned a specific reading from Haftorah/ Prophets to follow each parsha portion every Shabbat. However, those Haftorah readings will change when a certain *parsha* is read during a particular time of year. For example, when the parsha *Mishpatim* coincides with *Shabbat Shekalim* or *Rosh Chodesh*[9] Adar 1 (during leap years), the Haftorah portion will change.

Historically, the Haftorah portions were selected when Jews were forbidden by Greek rulers to read the Torah. The Haftorah was instituted to circumvent this Greek censorship and to ensure that Torah principles continued to be taught. Hence, you will notice a link between the Torah and the Haftorah selections so that the Torah's theme is taught through the Haftorah.

Each Shabbat has a Brit Chadasha portion (New Testament).

Found only in Messianic calendars, selected passages in the Brit Chadasha are connected with the *parsha* each week, thereby demonstrating the continuity of Scripture.

There are eight special Shabbatot (Sabbaths).[10]

Four Sabbaths have additional Torah readings, and four have an additional Haftorah reading. (*Shabbat Shirah* is noted below but it has no additional readings.)

9. Rosh Chodesh-head of the month or New Moon, the first of the Hebrew month

10. See Appendix B

The Four Parshiyot (parshas)

1. Shabbat Shekalim (shekels) is the Shabbat before Rosh Chodesh Adar[11]. This recalls the census taken in the wilderness (Ex 30:11-16).

Since counting the children of Israel was forbidden, the coins could be counted instead. The people were to donate a half shekel (a silver coin with a specific weight) as a tax to provide for the upkeep of the Tabernacle, and later the Temple. The tax also paid for the daily sacrifices; all of Israel shared equally in the worship and maintenance. The deposited coins were considered *hekdesh*[12] and were not permitted to be used for any other purpose. When the Temple stood and the people made the tri-annual pilgrimage to Jerusalem, it was easy to deposit the holy half shekel.

Although there is no Temple and no set standard to collect the half shekel, Reuven Prager, a Levite living in the land of Israel, is minting each year a pure silver half shekel according to the requirements. [13] This half shekel is being minted and collected in anticipation of the Third Temple. The nascent Sanhedrin in Israel has approved Prager's minting and collection of the half-shekel.

11. Adar – Hebrew month before Passover generally falls in either February or March

12. Hekdesh – sanctified

13. You can read more about the coin at the website www.begedivri.com.

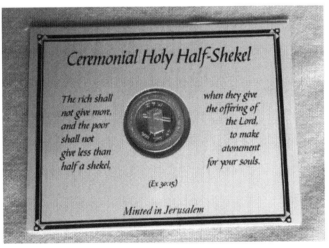

Ceremonial Holy Half-Shekel

The rich shall not give more, and the poor shall not give less than half a shekel.

when they give the offering of the Lord, to make atonement for your souls.

(Ex 30:15)

Minted in Jerusalem

Following Rosh HaShanah 2016, the Sanhedrin in Israel issued a Jubilee medallion which can be used in place of the actual silver half-shekel to perform the mitzvah. The advantage of this medallion is that since it represents the half-shekel, but is not the actual coin, it does not need to be deposited physically, and the funds are still set aside for Temple use.

The funds raised from the sale of the Sanhedrin medallions are dedicated to recreating the special vessels and utensils for Temple use and for priestly training. Unlike the silver half-shekel which is collected and held in safe-keeping until the Third Temple is constructed, the funds from the medallion sales are currently being used.

Traditionally, the value of a half shekel is given to charity on the Fast of Esther. As the value of silver fluctuates, it is difficult to render a precise equivalent, so some authorities suggest $5. In March of 2017 Chief Sephardi Rabbi of Israel, Rabbi Yitzack Yosef, set the current value of the half-shekel at 23 NIS (New Israeli Shekel) or $6.23. This half shekel is _not_ the poll tax referred to by Yeshua in Matthew chapters 17 and 22. That was a tax required to be paid per capita to the current ruler.

2. Shabbat Zachor (Sabbath of Remembrance) is the Shabbat before Purim. [14]

The portion read is Deuteronomy 25:17-19, which describes the attack by Amalek upon the Children of Israel as they left Egypt. Amalek attacked those who lagged behind because they were weary and faint from the journey. This would have most likely been the very young and old. We are commanded "...you shall blot out the memory of Amalek from under heaven; you must not forget."

Haman the Agagite was the King's confidante in the book of Esther who plotted to kill the Jews in Persia. The traditional understanding from the *Talmud*[15] is

14. Purim – "lots" festival recorded in the book of Esther.

15. For more information on the Jewish sources, see *Introduction to the Jewish Sources* by the author

Haman was a direct descendant of Agag, the king of the Amalekites (1 Samuel 15:9ff).

One does not have to look very far today to see modern "Hamans": Hitler, Mussolini, Stalin, and ISIS. May HaShem deliver us!

3. ***Shabbat Parah*** (the red heifer) is the Shabbat immediately following Purim.

The portion read is Numbers 19:1-22 which instructs in the preparation and use of the ashes of the red heifer (*parah adumah*) for purification, specifically from the impurity associated from contact with a corpse.   This marks the beginning of the formal preparations for Passover.

Passover is a time to cleanse not only our homes of leaven, but to examine ourselves for impurities. In ancient Israel those going up to Jerusalem would need to purify themselves by immersing in a *mikveh*[16] before going into the Temple.   The corresponding *haftarah* portion is Ezekiel 36:16-38, which also talks about purification.

There are strong similarities between Yeshua and the *parah adumah*. The red heifer requirements were that it must be unblemished and free of defect. The animal was sacrificed outside the camp and its blood was sprinkled seven times toward the Tent of Meeting. The applied ashes from the unblemished, no defect (perfect) red heifer cleansed an individual from all defilement.

That which was perfect made those who handled it ritually unclean until evening, yet the ashes mixed with water made ritually clean those who were unclean. Yeshua, our *Cohen HaGadol* (High Priest) who was perfect, was made unclean on our behalf:

16. Mikveh –
    ritual bath

For if the blood of goats and bulls
and the ashes of a heifer sprinkling

18

those who have been defiled,
sanctify for the cleansing of the flesh,
how much more will the blood of
Messiah, who through the eternal
Spirit offered Himself without blemish
to G-d, cleanse your conscience
from dead works to serve the living
G-d.[17]

4.   Shabbat HaChodesh (Sabbath of the Month).
This special Torah selection is read on the Shabbat
before Rosh Chodesh Nisan[18] (or if they coincide,
on Rosh Chodesh Nisan). The reading is Exodus 12:1-
20: *This month shall be for you the beginning of the
months; it shall be for you the first of the months of
the year* (Exodus 12:2). The corresponding haftarah
portion is Ezekiel 45:16-46:18, which also talks about
the first months and the offerings at that time.

The Hebrew calendar is thus established in regard to
counting the months, i.e., Nisan is "month one." The
years, however, are calculated from Rosh HaShanah,
or 1 Tishrei[19].

Other Special Shabbatot

These Sabbaths receive special notice on the
calendar because either they have special Haftorah
readings, or they have special significance in regard
to their respective standard readings. They do not
have special Torah readings.

Shabbat Shirah (Sabbath of Song) does not have an
additional reading, but it is the Shabbat when we
read the *parsha Beshalach* (Exodus 13:17-17:16).
This *parsha* includes the Song at the Sea – praises
which were sung by the Israelites after the Egyptians
had drowned in the Sea of Reeds (Red Sea). In
some synagogues this song is chanted in a special
trop (cantillation). Since the parting of the sea is
celebrated as a great miracle and the climactic
episode to the exodus from Egypt, the Song at the

17. He 9:13-14

18. Nisan-
Hebrew month
where Passover
occurs (Mar-Apr)

19. Tishrei-
Hebrew month
where Rosh
Hashanah
occurs (Sept-
Oct)

19

Sea has become associated with thanksgiving and praise.

Jewish tradition teaches that there are only ten true songs (Shirot) in the history of the world. They are more than melodies; they are expressions of the harmony of creation and mark monumental transitions in Jewish history.

The Haftorah portion also contains another one of these songs, the Song of Deborah (Judges 5:1-31). The sages teach that the tenth and final song has not yet been sung; it is the Song of the coming of Messiah which will be sung at the end of days (Isaiah 26:1).

Shabbat HaGadol (the Great Sabbath) is the Shabbat before Passover. Generally, rabbis will teach about Passover preparations as part of their sermons. It commemorates the 10th of Nisan when Israelites took the lambs they had chosen to sacrifice for Pesach and staked them outside of their homes. These lambs would be examined for any defect, blemish, or sickness before they were offered. At the time of the Exodus, this was a dangerous practice because the Egyptians worshiped sheep. But, again, HaShem preserved Israel.

Yeshua most likely entered Jerusalem on the 10th of Nisan riding a donkey, fulfilling the Messianic prophecy found in Zechariah 9:9. For the next few days Yeshua was observed, questioned, (Matthew 21:23-27), tested, and found without blemish. After examining him, Pilate said of Yeshua, "I find no fault in this man" (Luke 23:4 KJV). See also Mark 14:53-65. Yochanan the Immerser (John the Baptist) testified in John 1:29, "Behold, the Lamb of G-d who takes away the sin of the world." Yeshua is the Passover Lamb.

The special Haftorah reading is Malachi 3:4-24, which is a Messianic prophecy regarding the end of days and the return of the prophet Elijah. Tradition is that Elijah will return at Pesach, so a place is set for him at the Seder table, usually with a special cup at his place setting just for his use. Following after the meal and the drinking of the third cup of wine, children open the door wide and call for Eliyahu (Elijah). The open door indicates that it is *leil shimurim,* "a night which enjoys the protection of HaShem." Jews who open the door while living in hostile places are certainly acting in trust for the Holy One.

Shabbat Chazon (Sabbath of Vision) is the Shabbat preceding Tisha B'Av (the 9th of Av) and refers to Isaiah's vision of the destruction of the Temple. The Haftorah reading is Isaiah 1:1-27. The 9th of Av is a fast day in remembrance and mourning for the destruction of both First and Second Temples.

In Jewish tradition, the 9th of Av problems began when Israel believed the report of the spies in Numbers 13 and 14 and refused to trust HaShem to keep them safe in the land promised to Israel. Throughout Israelite history, there have been tragedies associated with this date.

Shabbat Nachamu (Sabbath of Consolation) is the Shabbat that follows Tisha B'Av. This is the first of seven Haftorah portions that lead up to Rosh Hashanah. These readings are meant to console Israel after the destruction of the Temple and to assure that HaShem will indeed build the Temple again.

Shabbat Shuvah (Sabbath of Return) is a play on the words "Shabbat Teshuvah," Sabbath of Repentance. This Shabbat is between Rosh Hashanah and Yom Kippur. It is a time for self-reflection and obviously, correction as individuals prepare themselves for the atonement of Yom Kippur.

There are two Haftorah readings for this day. The first is Hosea 14:2-10, which addresses the need for sincere repentance and acknowledgement of

HaShem's great mercy and subsequent restoration. The other selection, Micah 7:18-20, speaks of HaShem's unchanging love and His desire and delight to forgive our sins.

All festival days, including Shabbat, begin at sundown on the day before. For example, Erev Shabbat begins Friday evening. This is because the first chapter of Genesis reads, "...and there was evening and morning, one day." This is extremely important for understanding when the Shabbat restrictions apply and when to celebrate. For example, the first day of Hanukkah actually begins at sundown the day before, and that is when to kindle the Hanukkah lights.

Havdalah הבדלה

Havdalah means separation or distinction, and it is the ritual that acknowledges the close of the holiness of Shabbat and the beginning of the mundane work week. Havdalah also is used to show the distinction of levels of holiness between Shabbat and other festival days.

Just as the candle lighting, wine, challah, songs, and prayers ushered in the weekly Sabbath and sanctified the time as holy, now the candle lighting, wine, songs, and prayers designate that the holy time of Shabbat has come to a close and it is time to return to the mundane work week. The words "holy" and "mundane" show the distinction between the times.

Once the sun has set Saturday evening (some will wait until three small stars are visible in the sky), the family lights a braided six- wicked candle (specifically for havdalah). Similar to Erev Shabbat, one pours a cup of wine, but for Havdalah, a container of sweet spices accompanies the fruit of the vine. The family says blessings and sings songs recognizing the distinction between the holy rest of Shabbat and the time following where work is expected. Here is the usual order of Havdalah:

1. A cup of wine is poured so that it overflows onto the plate beneath it. The overflowed wine symbolizes abundance and blessing.

2. The Havdalah candle is lit. If you do not have a specific Havdalah candle, hold two lit candles together so that their flames are touching. This large flame represents the fire that Adam started following Shabbat. Read Isaiah 12:2-3, Psalms 3:8, 46:11, 84:12, 20:9, Esther 8:16, Psalm 116:13.

3. Say the blessing over the upraised cup of wine. *"Blessed are You, Adonai, Eloheinu, King of the universe, Who creates the fruit of the vine."* The upraised cup is called the Cup of Salvation. Express gratitude to HaShem, and lift a cup of wine symbolizing the joy of salvation.

4. Pass around the spice box, or smell a jar of kitchen spices such as cloves, cinnamon, allspice, or apple pie spice. After all present have had an opportunity to smell the spices, the following blessing is said. *"Blessed are You, Adonai Eloheinu, King of the universe, Who creates species of fragrance."* There are several reasons given for the smelling of the fragrant spices at the end of Shabbat. As we smell the spices, we are reminded of the pleasantness of Shabbat and it comforts the soul as Shabbat comes to a close.

5. Pronounce the blessing over the lighted candles. *"Blessed are You, Adonai Eloheinu, King of the universe, Who creates the illuminations of fire."* Hold up fingers to the flame and gaze upon the reflected light. Just as Adam was grateful for the light, so are believers in Yeshua grateful for the illumination the Holy One gives.

6. The final blessing is the Havdalah (separation). This blessing defines the separation between the holiness of Shabbat and the other days of the week. Say, *"Blessed are You, Adonai Eloheinu, King of the universe, Who separates between holy and secular, between light and darkness, between Israel and the nations, between the seventh day and the six days of labor. Blessed are You, HaShem, Who separates between holy and secular."*

7. The one who recited Havdalah, or someone else present, should drink most, but not all, of the wine from the cup. The remainder of the wine is used to extinguish the flame, which is held over a plate. It is the custom of many to dip the fingers into the wine-covered dish and touch the eyelids and inner pockets with them. This symbolizes that the "light of the commandments" will guide all through the week.

8. This is followed by *zemirot* (songs); the best known is "Eliyahu Hanavi" (Elijah the prophet). *"Elijah the prophet, Elijah the Tishbi, Elijah the Giladi. May he quickly come to us with Messiah, son of David."*

9. End Havdalah by greeting one another with the words *"Shavuah Tov!"* "Good week!"

SEVEN MOEDIM

These seven *moedim* (festival days) correspond to seven High Shabbats (Holy Days). These days are kept as Shabbatot whether the day falls on a weekly Sabbath or not. With the exclusion of food preparation and cooking (for some), these days carry the same restrictions as a weekly Shabbat. They are Passover, Unleavened Bread, First Fruits, Pentecost, Trumpets, Day of Atonement, and Tabernacles. As with many things Biblical, some of these feast days are often called by their Hebrew names or Jewish nicknames. For a concise chart of the Hebrew months, their English equivalents, and the corresponding moedim, see Appendix C.

Passover	Unleavened Bread	Firstfruits of the Barley
Pesach	Chag HaMatzah	Yom HaBikkurim

Pentecost	Trumpets	Atonements	Tabernacles
Weeks	Yom Teruah	Yom Kippur	Sukkot
Shavuot	Rosh HaShanah	Yom HaKippurim	Booths
			Ingathering or Asiph

SPRING FESTIVALS

Passover   פסח

Passover is the first of the three pilgrimage festivals for which Israel is commanded to travel up to Jerusalem. It is a liberation festival celebrating release from slavery in Egypt so that Israel could serve G-d freely.

During the tenth and final plague HaShem brought upon Egypt, He passed over the Israelites and struck down all the firstborn in Egypt. It was after this night that Pharaoh relented and finally freed the Hebrews. Since then, Israel gathers on that night to commemorate that time and to contemplate what it means to be delivered by signs and wonders, by war, and by a mighty hand and outstretched arm.

This is not just a remembrance, but the Jewish sages say each person is to see himself or herself today as again standing with loins girded, staff in hand, and ready to go:

> ...You are a chosen race, a royal priesthood, a holy nation, a people for G-d's own possession, that you may proclaim the excellencies

of Him who has called you out of
darkness into His marvelous light.[20]

Israelites remove all of the leaven from their homes
prior to Passover and do not consume any leaven
from 14 Nisan at dark until the 21st day of Nisan at
sunset:

> In the first month, on the fourteenth
> day of the month at twilight is the
> L-rd's Passover.

On the fifteenth day of the same month, there is the
Feast of Unleavened Bread to the L-rd:

> For seven days you shall eat
> unleavened bread.[21]

In Jewish homes on the first night of Passover the family
gathers for a festive meal called a Seder ("order").
The meal is much more than just a liturgical service.
Songs, prayers and certain elements involving all five
senses tell the story of the Exodus from Egypt. Young
and old alike meaningfully participate. A Passover
meal (seder) is what Messiah Yeshua and his
talmidim[22] celebrated, although it is a ritual taught
in Christian circles as The Last Supper or Communion.

The scripture says:

> And when He had taken a cup
> and given thanks, He said, 'Take
> this and share it among yourselves;
> for I say to you, I will not drink of the
> fruit of the vine from now on until
> the kingdom of G-d comes.' And
> when He had taken some bread
> and given thanks, He broke it, and
> gave it to them, saying, 'This is My
> body which is given for you; **do this** in
> **remembrance** of Me.'[23]

20. De 4:34 and I
Pe 2:9

21. Le 23:5-6

22. Talmidim -
disciples

23. Lu 22:17-
19 (emphasis
added)

29

I gently ask the question: What is the **"this"** by which believers are to remember Yeshua, Communion or Passover? The answer is the Passover Seder.

On the Seder plate are several elements.

- A bowl of salt water, *Mi Malach,* symbolizes the bitter tears shed while enslaved.
- The roasted egg, *Beitzah,* commemorates the Passover offering brought to the Temple in Jerusalem. It is also a symbol of renewal.
- Parsley, *Karpas,* is symbolic of the hyssop used to place the blood over the doorposts and lintels.
- The roasted shank bone, *z'roah,* symbolizes the lamb the Hebrews sacrificed and ate in Temple times, and it is a reminder that HaShem "passed over" the homes of the Israelites and spared the firstborn during the tenth plague. *Z'roah* is translated as "limb" or "upper arm." It is the Arm of HaShem (Yeshua).
- *Charoset,* a mixture of apples, honey, nuts, wine and spices that resemble mortar, symbolizing the mortar that the Hebrews had to make for the bricks in Egypt. In other Jewish communities around the world, the *charoset* may be made from fruits found in the local area, e.g., dates, bananas and figs. For a basic recipe, see Appendix D.
- *Maror* is bitter herbs. Usually horseradish is used. The *maror* is a reminder of how bitter the Egyptians made the lives of the Hebrews by enslaving them.
- The *matzah*[24] is the unleavened bread, oftentimes called the bread of affliction. It is the symbol of how the Israelites had to leave Egypt in such haste that the dough did not have time to rise. It is striped and pierced like Messiah, and it is without leaven. It is broken during the Seder, and one part (the *afikomen*)[25]

24. Passover matzah is made of wheat that has not had any moisture come in contact with it prior to preparation for baking. Otherwise the wheat flour would be rendered unfit for consumption during Passover.

25. Afikomen- literal translation lost in antiquity. Some say it means, "I have come others" others say "dessert".

is wrapped in a white cloth and hidden away to be redeemed after the meal.

It is after the eating of the festive meal (*Shulchan Orech*) that children search for the the *afikomen* and their parents ransom it. Notably, the *afikomen* is eaten during the part of the Seder known as *Tzafun*, which means hidden or concealed. This is a hidden picture of Messiah during the Seder service. Since all are commanded to see themselves in Egypt with loins girded and staff in hand, all eat this *afikomen* seeing themselves at the precipice of deliverance.

In some Messianic congregations, part of the tradition is to pray individually for specific deliverance and healing before eating the *afikomen*. Before this night, HaShem has used relationships and circumstances to reveal to each person what he or she needs for deliverance. His Word says that when Israel left Egypt, not one person stumbled. That is an awesome statement considering the crushing type of work the Hebrew slaves performed in Egypt.

> He also struck down all the firstborn in their land, the first fruits of all their vigor. Then He brought them out with silver and gold; **and among His tribes there was not one who stumbled.**[26]

Yeshua, the Passover Lamb, led Israel out then, and He leads Israel out today, strengthening the weak and infusing courage to the fearful.

There has been miraculous healing and deliverance at this author's Seders. As HaShem told Joshua:

> **Be strong** and courageous, for you shall give this people possession of the land which I swore to their fathers to give them. Only **be strong** and very courageous; be careful to

26. Ps 105:36-37 (emphasis added)

31

do according to all the law which Moses My servant commanded you; do not turn from it to the right or to the left, so that you may have success wherever you go. This book of the law shall not depart from your mouth, but you shall meditate on it day and night, so that you may be careful to do according to all that is written in it; for then you will make your way prosperous, and then you will have success.   Have I not commanded you? **Be strong** and courageous! Do not tremble or be dismayed, for the L-RD your G-d is with you wherever you go.[27]

Stand fast and keep the commandments.   Israel's Commander in Chief stands with us and fights for us.

And He caused their chariot wheels to swerve, and He made them drive with difficulty; so the Egyptians said, 'Let us flee from Israel, for the L-rd is **fighting for them** against the Egyptians.' [28]

Unleavened Bread חג המצות

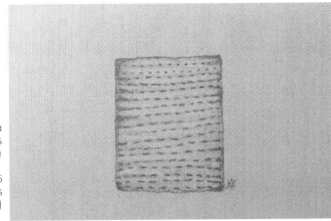

27. Joshua 1:6-9 (emphasis added)

28. Ex 14:25 (emphasis added)

Passover is celebrated only one night, but Unleavened Bread is seven days.

> In the first month, on the fourteenth day of the month at twilight is the L-rd's Passover. Then on the fifteenth day of the same month there is the Feast of Unleavened Bread to the L-rd; for seven days you shall eat unleavened bread.[29]

Since matzah is eaten on Passover, the two holidays are almost always called collectively "Passover."

There are many reasons given for eating unleavened bread. Yeshua gives some hints about leaven:

> Then they understood that He did not say to beware of the leaven of bread, but of the teaching of the Pharisees and Sadducees.[30]

Paul instructed the Corinthians in 1 Corinthians 5:7-8:

> Clean out the old leaven that you may be a new lump, just as you are in fact unleavened. For Messiah our Passover also has been sacrificed. Let us therefore celebrate the feast, not with old leaven, nor with the leaven of malice and wickedness, but with the unleavened bread of sincerity and truth.

Eating matzah, or unleavened bread, is not just about dietary restrictions. In fact, it is a call to examine for and cleanse both our homes and ourselves from leaven. Everyone needs to remove hypocrisy, bad attitudes, religious ideology, deception, illusion, evil, deceit, etc., from his or her life. Each individual should expect to be different each year as he or she comes to the Passover table.

29. Le 23:5-6

30. Mt 16:12

33

One of the rituals that helps children to see the correlation between the physical and spiritual is *bedikat chametz*, the search (inspection) for leaven. The nightfall before Passover, after the whole house has been cleaned, the family says a blessing and begins the search for any leaven. The blessing is:

> Blessed are You, Adonai,
> Eloheinu, King of the Universe,
> who has sanctified us through His
> commandments, commanding us to
> remove all chametz."[31]

Usually the mother will leave a small amount of chametz (leaven) where it can be found easily and removed. Using a *bedikat chametz* kit, the parents, along with the children, go through each room with a candle (remember, it's dark), a feather, and a wooden spoon looking for any "unfound" leaven. Obviously, some purposefully has been left to be found.

Once located, the leaven is brushed onto the spoon or into a bag using the feather. The items are taken outside, and the next morning the leaven is burned in its entirety. This demonstrates to children that even when one thinks that all leaven has been removed, there is still something there. Believers need the illumination of the *Ruach HaKodesh* (Holy Spirit) to help find that hidden place that needs cleansing. Just as a feather gently removes the leaven, believers can trust the Heavenly Father to gently remove the leaven from their lives if they are willing to participate in the search and are open to allowing Him to completely eradicate it.

After the "found" leaven is set aside to be burned in the morning, one says the following:

> Any chametz or leaven that is in my
> possession which I have not seen,
> have not removed and do not know

31. Chametz – leaven. Any food made with wheat, barley, oats, rye or spelt.

about, may it be annulled and become ownerless, like the dust of the earth.

This declaration does not exempt anyone from searching out or cleaning away the leaven, rather it is an affirmation of HaShem's love and mercy.

Yom HaBikkurim/First Fruits יום הבכורים

Speak to the sons of Israel, and say to them, 'When you enter the land which I am going to give to you and reap its harvest, then you shall bring in the sheaf of the **first fruits** of your harvest to the priest. And he shall wave the sheaf before the L-rd for you to be accepted; on the day after the Sabbath the priest shall wave it.' [32]

In ancient Israel when the Temple stood, Jews brought the first fruits of their produce from Eretz Yisrael[33] to the Temple. The minimum that would be brought was 1/60 of their crops. Those who lived

32. Leviticus 23:10-11

33. Eretz Yisrael- the land of Israel

closest to Jerusalem would bring fresh fruit or grain, and those who lived further away brought dried. The baskets in which the produce was carried to Jerusalem also were given to the priests.

The specifically-commanded first fruits was the seven species found in the Land, which are wheat, barley, dates (honey), pomegranate, figs, grapes (wine) and olives (oil). Deuteronomy 26:1-11 would be recited before the individual would turn his offering over to the priest. This was a declaration of HaShem's faithfulness to deliver Israel from Egypt and to bring them into the Promised Land. The evidence of His faithfulness was the produce in hand.

The Brit Chadasha reads: "But now Messiah has been raised from the dead, the **first fruits** of those who are asleep"[34] again, testifying to HaShem's faithfulness to resurrect those who are asleep in Him. Yeshua's death and resurrection brought Israel out of bondage to the kingdom of darkness. The ongoing promise is that as one walks in obedience, HaShem will continue to restore, and the individual will continue to take back the ground that had once been surrendered.

Shavuot/Feast of Weeks חג שבעת

34. 1 Corinthians 15:20 (emphasis added)

Shavuot literally means "weeks," and it is the second pilgrimage festival. Israel is commanded in Exodus 34:22:

> And you shall celebrate the Feast of Weeks, that is, the first fruits of the wheat harvest, and the Feast of Ingathering at the turn of the year;

and in Leviticus 23:15-16:

> You shall also count for yourselves from the day after the sabbath, from the day when you brought in the sheaf of the wave offering, there shall be seven complete sabbaths. You shall count fifty days to the day after the seventh sabbath; then you shall present a new grain offering to the L-RD.

The count to Shavuot starts on the 15th of Nisan, which usually is the second night of Seder. That count concludes on Sivan 6, Shavuot. There are multiple reasons within the tradition for counting the days, but the most straightforward is anticipation and preparation for the event of Shavuot. These days of counting are called the Omer. [35] You can read the instructions for the Omer under Additional Information.

The culmination of Shavuot is the giving of the Torah on Mount Sinai. Israel willingly binds herself to the covenant and becomes HaShem's people. The Christian church calls this Pentecost, the Greek word meaning fifty:

35. Omer was a specified measure taken from the new wheat crop that had been harvested the second night of Passover to be brought to the Temple as a special offering.

> And when the day of Pentecost had come, they were all together in one place. And suddenly there came from heaven a noise like a violent, rushing wind, and it filled the whole

house where they were sitting. And
there appeared to them tongues as
of fire distributing themselves, and
they rested on each one of them.
And they were all filled with the Holy
Spirit and began to speak with other
tongues, as the Spirit was giving
them utterance.[36]

Just as the Ruach[37] set the tongues of fire upon
their head, so did HaShem set His voice (which could
be seen) upon Israel at Mount Sinai.

One of the most beautiful images of Shavuot is that
of the marriage between HaShem (groom) and
Israel (bride). Part of the liturgy is the reading of a
ketubah[38] between HaShem and His people. The
book of Ruth is read in the synagogue, which is a
picture of the stranger coming to trust in the G-d of
Israel and joining herself to not only the G-d of Israel,
but His people as well.

Specific instructions were given to prepare for this
festival, and they are found in Exodus 19:10-15:

36. Acts 2:1-4

37. Ruach - spirit

38. Ketubah –
literally, "a thing
written", is a
legally binding
document
read before
the wedding
ceremony takes
place which
stipulates what
the husband's
rights and
responsibilities
are toward his
wife; similar to
a modern day
pre-nuptial
agreement.

The L-rd also said to Moses, 'Go to
the people and consecrate them
today and tomorrow, and let them
wash their garments; and let them
be ready for the third day, for on the
third day the L-rd will come down
on Mount Sinai in the sight of all the
people. And you shall set bounds
for the people all around, saying,
"'Beware that you do not go up on
the mountain or touch the border of
it; whoever touches the mountain
shall surely be put to death. No
hand shall touch him, but he shall
surely be stoned or shot through;
whether beast or man, he shall not
live.'" When the ram's horn sounds

a long blast, they shall come up to the mountain. So Moses went down from the mountain to the people and consecrated the people, and they washed their garments. And he said to the people, 'Be ready for the third day; do not go near a woman.'

Further instruction is in Leviticus 23:15-23.

…You shall bring in from your dwelling places two loaves of bread for a wave offering, made of two-tenths ephah; they shall be baked with leaven as first fruits to the L-rd…

Some of the customs of this holiday are to eat dairy foods and decorate the synagogue with flowers and greenery. The flowers and greenery are reminiscent of the foliage on Mt Sinai. There are multiple reasons for why the custom is to eat a dairy meal on Shavuot. Some say it is because Jews had just received the laws of kashrut[39] and none of the cooking pots or prepared meat met the kosher requirements. Some individuals eat dairy foods with honey in them because the Torah is likened to milk and honey: "Honey and milk are under your tongue.[40]"

FALL FESTIVALS

The themes of the fall festivals are repentance, judgment, and atonement. During this time, believers carefully examine themselves: in the light of whom we wish to be, who are we really today? In what ways have we failed others, ourselves, and even HaShem? This introspection is meant to lead each person to acknowledge what he has done, feel regret and remorse for doing it, and to attempt restitution when possible.

In Judaism, it is not enough to confess one's sins before G-d. If one has hurt others, he is to make an

39. Kashrut-kosher

40. Song of Songs 4:11

effort to repent to the offended or injured party, and if possible, to make restitution. One chooses to turn away from past sinful behavior and make a sincere effort to change by acting accordingly in the New Year. Real repentance starts inside the heart, and it is reflected outwardly in deeds. The outward good deeds are no longer something the person does, but rather who he has become.

The entire month of Elul[41], the month before Rosh HaShanah, is characterized by the blowing of a shofar daily in the synagogue. It is calling people to repentance and sounding confusion to Satan and his army.

Rosh Hashanah Yom Teruah יום תרועה

41. Elul – Hebrew month before Rosh HaShanah Aug-Sept

42. Tishrei – Hebrew month occurring Sept-Oct

43. Diaspora – land other than Israel

Yom Teruah, the day of blowing the shofar, is also known as Rosh HaShanah, which means "head of the year." Yom Teruah occurs on 1 Tishrei[42] and is celebrated for two days in the diaspora.[43] Leviticus 23:24-25:

> Speak to the sons of Israel, saying, in the seventh month on the first of the month, you shall have a rest, a reminder by blowing of trumpets,

a holy convocation. You shall not
do any laborious work, but you shall
present an offering by fire to the
L-RD.

The synagogue is the focal place for observance of
Rosh Hashanah. The liturgy's main theme is that G-d
is King, and as the One who created the whole world,
He continues to renew His creation. The Scripture
readings on this day, the rabbis say, reflect three
major principles: (1) acceptance and declaration
of HaShem as G-d and King of the universe; (2)
acknowledgment that HaShem intervenes in the
world, and He will punish the wicked and reward
the righteous; (3) recognition that HaShem revealed
Himself and His Torah at Mount Sinai, and He will fully
reveal Himself again to bring about the end of days.

Rosh HaShanah is considered the birthday of the
world. This day is a solemn one because it is a time of
judgment, so individuals consider every action and
thought, and yet there is a confidence that HaShem
is merciful and will judge accordingly if he or she
repents.

On the afternoon of Rosh HaShanah, it is customary
to go to a body of water where there are living fish.
The practice of throwing bread crumbs into the
water comes from Micah 7:19:

> He will again have compassion on
> us; He will tread our iniquities under
> foot. Yes, Thou wilt <u>cast all their sins
> into the depths of the sea.</u>

At the water's edge one says the *Tashlich*[44] prayer,
which comes from Micah 7:17-20:

> Who, O G-d is like you, Who pardons
> iniquity, and overlooks transgression
> for the remnant of His heritage? Who
> has not retained His wrath eternally,

44. Tashlich-
literally "to cast"
found in Micah
7:19

41

for He desires kindness! He will again
be merciful to us; He will suppress our
iniquities. And cast into the depths
of the sea all their sins. Grant truth to
Jacob, kindness to Abraham, as You
swore to our forefathers from ancient
times.

Next is a prayer from Psalm 118:5-9:

From the straits did I call upon G-d,
He answered me with expansiveness.
HaShem is with me, I have no fear-
how can man affect me? HaShem
is with me, through my helpers,
therefore I can face my foes. It is
better to take refuge in HaShem
than to rely on man. It is better to
take refuge in HaShem than to rely
on nobles.

Other psalms to read are Psalm 33 and 130.

As each person casts those bread crumbs (or lint
from a pocket) into the water, they see HaShem
carrying their sins far away and remembering them
no more. Psalm 103:12 states:

As far as the east is from the
west, so far has He removed our
transgressions from us...

The rabbis say one is required to *hear* the shofar
sound 100 times on Rosh HaShanah. The requirement
is not to blow, but to hear.   There are four specific
sounds that are blown: *tekiah, shevarim, teruah,
tekiah gedolah.*

Tekiah is a long, clear, unwavering
sound. This sound is placed at the
beginning and end of the series of
shofar calls like bookends. It is the

sound to awaken the slumberer from his sleep so he or she will pay attention to the next sounds that follow.

Shevarim are three short, wavering blasts. They represent the weeping and wailing of mourning. The sounds are fractured, and they represent each individual who cries out to HaShem from life's tragedies and disappointments.

Teruah are nine short, staccato blasts, the sound of battle and warfare. The hearer is no longer complacent, for the previous sounds have awakened, and now all are called to action. The repentant one must change.

Tekiah Gedolah is one very long clear and distinct sound. It was the final sound heard on Yom Kippur to signal that the sacrifice and prayers had been received. The final trump! It is a signal that HaShem is unwavering, consistent and strong. All who keep His command and follow Him can aspire to that.

Yamim Noraim יָמִים נוֹרָאִים

Yamim Noraim is a ten-day period from Rosh Hashanah to the conclusion of Yom Kippur known as The Days of Awe. It is a time of great reflection and repentance.

Tradition teaches that HaShem has books in which names are recorded; the books indicate who will live and who will die, who will have a difficult life, or who will have a good life in the coming year. These books are written on Rosh HaShanah, but one's actions during Yamim Noraim can alter HaShem's decrees.

Teshuvah (sincere turning away from sin), *tefilah* (prayer), and *tzedekah* (good deeds, including charity) can change the outcome. No one is spiritually without need of improvement. The books are then sealed on Yom Kippur.

The prayer on Rosh HaShanah regarding this is:

> On Rosh HaShanah it is written, on Yom Kippur it is sealed: how many shall pass on, how many shall come to be; who shall live and who shall die; who shall see ripe age and who will not; who will perish by fire and who by water; who by sword and who by beasts; who by hunger and who by thirst; who by earthquake and who by plague; who by strangling and who by stoning; who shall be secure and who shall be driven; who shall be tranquil and who shall be troubled; who shall be poor and who shall be rich; who shall be humbled and who shall be exalted; but repentance, prayer and righteousness temper judgment's severe decrees.

Since the names are written in books, the traditional greeting during this time is *l'shanah tovah* ("for a good year"). This is a shortening of *"l'shanah tovah tikatev v'taihatem"* (or to women, *"l'shanah tovah tikatevi v'taihatemi"*), which means "May you be inscribed and sealed [in the Book of Life] for a good year."

Apples dipped in honey to symbolize the desire for a good, sweet year yielding good fruit are eaten.

Yom Kippur יום כפר

Yom Kippur is the Day of Atonement occurring on the tenth of Tishrei.

> And this shall be a permanent
> statute for you: in the seventh month,
> on the tenth day of the month, you
> shall humble your souls, and not do
> any work, whether the native, or the
> alien who sojourns among you; for
> it is on this day that atonement shall
> be made for you to cleanse you;
> you shall be clean from all your sins
> before the L-rd. It is to be a sabbath
> of solemn rest for you, that you may
> humble your souls; it is a permanent
> statute.[45]

Yom Kippur is considered the holiest day of the year. Even marginally observant Jews will be found fasting and praying in a synagogue. Yom Kippur is for atonement for sins between the individual and HaShem. Sins between an individual and another person are to be repented of, the wrongs righted (if they can be), and reconciliation made -- all prior to Yom Kippur.

45. Le 16:28-30

Yom Kippur is a complete Sabbath. No work is done, nor may one eat or drink (not even water). It is a complete fast from sunset on the evening before until after nightfall on Yom Kippur day.

Since the Scriptures command Israel to afflict/ humble themselves on this day, the *Talmud* also specifies additional restrictions:

- do not bathe or anoint the body
- wear no makeup, deodorant, body oil, etc...
- abstain from marital relations
- in the desire not to remind HaShem of the incident with the golden calf, one doesn't wear leather into the sanctuary; instead, canvas sneakers or other types of materials used for footwear are worn.

There is a custom of Jewish males wearing white on Yom Kippur. A *kittel* (a white robe) goes over the clothes. Because it is similar to a burial shroud, one is reminded of his own mortality and the need to repent and do *teshuvah*. Believers in Messiah are reminded that although our sins may be as scarlet, they will become white as snow, as it says in Isaiah 1:18.

Since the commandments found in Torah are all about life, restrictions may be lifted if there is a threat to the life or health of an individual. Children under the age of nine do not fast; neither do women in labor up to and including three days postpartum. In illness, the fast may also be broken.

Sukkot סכות

Sukkot, literally meaning "booths," is also known as the Feast of Tabernacles and occurs on the 15th of Tishrei. This is the third of the three pilgrimage festivals.

Sukkot lasts for seven days from the 15th of Tishrei to the 21st of Tishrei. The first day and the eighth day are Shabbatot. Like Pesach and Shavuot, it is an agriculturally-based festival -- this one following after all of the harvest has been brought in:

> On exactly the fifteenth day of the seventh month, when you have gathered in the crops of the land, you shall celebrate the feast of the L-rd for seven days, with a rest on the first day and a rest on the eighth day.[46]

There are three commandments associated with this festival.

1. **Sukkah**. The first is the sukkah, or booth, that families construct and dwell in for seven days. This temporary structure is reminiscent of the booths Israel lived in during the desert wanderings. It is not a symbol of privation, but one of trust, as HaShem kept His people safe from harm (animals, scorpions, snakes, weather, enemies) in them as they traveled.

46. Le 23:39

The Talmud requires a roof that is not entirely closed, but one where one can view the stars. The roof materials must be raw, unfinished, "living" materials (not plastic or metal). Corn stalks, bamboo poles, branches from evergreen trees, reeds, narrow strips of "raw" wood that is not painted or varnished, etc., may be used. Often people use the wooden strips and place greenery on top, although the wooden strips are acceptable alone.

The structure can have windows and a door, but it must be temporary. This means that if it is attached to the home or porch, it must be able to be dismantled after the holiday:

> You shall live in booths for seven days; all the native-born in Israel shall live in booths, so that your generations may know that I had the sons of Israel live in booths when I brought them out from the land of Egypt. I am the L-rd your G-d.[47]

2. **Four Species.** The second commandment concerns instructions for gathering the four species, called *arba minim*, also called the *lulav* and *etrog*:

> Now on the first day you shall take for yourselves the foliage of beautiful trees, palm branches and boughs of leafy trees and willows of the brook; and you shall rejoice before the L-rd your G-d for seven days.[48]

The four species emphasize the agricultural basis of Sukkot. This holiday comes after the final harvest and prior to winter. It makes sense that Israel would gather and bind together, four beautiful kinds of living things and use them to thank HaShem for the bountiful harvest.

47. Le 23:42-43

48. Le 23:40

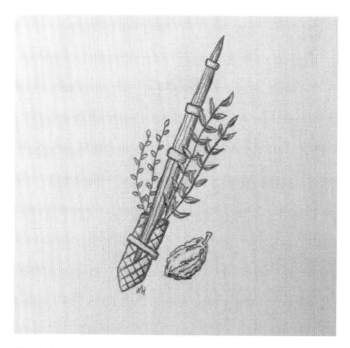

The lulav consists of a woven palm holder where an unopened palm branch is placed in the middle slot, two willows (aravot) are placed in the left slot, and to the right are three myrtles (hadasim).

The etrog, a lemon about the size of a fist, is not attached with the other three species, but is held in the hand along with the lulav. The lulav and etrog are held together, and as blessings are recited, they are shaken in six directions -- south, north, east, up, down and west. They are shaken vertically, pointing upward to heaven and shaken with the bottom pointing down. The top of the lulav is never pointed downward. The etrog represents the heart, life, and energy, all to be used in service to the King.

The palm branch is stiff. It represents the spine and fortitude with which to serve HaShem with patience and courage. The willow has leaves shaped like the mouth, representing speech before HaShem -- blessing instead of cursing. The myrtle has leaves shaped like an eye, representing insight and discernment (how we perceive the inner nature of a thing), intuition, and wisdom.

3. **Rejoice!** The third commandment is to rejoice:

> ...and you shall rejoice before the
> L-rd your G-d for seven days.[49]

Many will host sukkah parties, inviting friends and family to sit in their sukkah and share some food. Some will also sing and play games. Since the commandment is to rejoice, the rabbis say one may be inside if the weather is not conducive to enjoy being in the sukkah. No one is rejoicing when sitting, sleeping, or eating in the rain!

Other Sukkot Traditions and Rituals

The first night of Sukkot, a blessing is made in the sukkah:

> Blessed are You, Adonai,
> Eloheinu, King of the universe,
> Who has sanctified us with His
> commandments and commanded
> us to live in the sukkah.

Next, candles are lit in the sukkah, and the *Shehecheyanu* blessing is made:

> Blessed are You, Adonai, Eloheinu,
> King of the universe, who has kept us
> alive and sustained us to reach this
> season.

49. Le 23:40

50. A recipe for challah is included in the back of the booklet

This last blessing refers to both the first day of the festival of Sukkot and the first use of the sukkah. Two loaves of challah[50] follow, just like on Shabbat.

There is a custom of inviting *ushpizin*, symbolic guests each day to join the family in the sukkah. These honorary guests may include Abraham, Sarah, Isaac, Rebecca, Jacob, Rachel, Leah, Joseph, Moses, Miriam, Aaron, King David, Abigail, and Queen Esther. A guest or more each day is invited to the sukkah[51].

There is a connection between the ushpizin and Sukkot. All of the ushpizin were wanderers, or exiles. Abraham left his home to travel to Canaan; Jacob fled Laban; Joseph was exiled into Egypt; Moses fled to Midian from Egypt; Miriam and her two brothers wandered in the desert; David fled from King Saul; and Esther lived in Persia. The theme of becoming sojourners in the earth is a theme repeated in the Brit Chadasha, and it is an important spiritual foundation of faith, for it reminds each believer to live in expectation of Messiah's return.

For believers in Messiah Yeshua, Sukkot is the traditional day of Yeshua's birth. His first act of obedience to Torah was his circumcision on the eighth day, which falls on Shemini Atzeret/Simcha Torah[52].

For the future, the prophet Zechariah says that if the nations don't keep the festival of Sukkot, then they will have no rain in their land:

> Then it will come about that any who
> are left of all the nations that went
> against Jerusalem will go up from
> year to year to worship the King,
> the L-rd of hosts, and to celebrate
> the Feast of Booths. And it will be
> that whichever of the families of the
> earth does not go up to Jerusalem
> to worship the King, the L-rd of hosts,
> there will be **no rain** on them. And if
> the family of Egypt does not go up or
> enter, then **no rain** will fall on them;
> it will be the plague with which the
> L-rd smites the nations who do not
> go up to celebrate the Feast of

51. For more information on the symbolism, spiritual attributes, and prophetic implications of the ushpizin and Shemini Atzeret, see BEKY Booklet *The Seven Shepherds: Hanukkah in Prophecy* by H. Alewine.

52. Shemini Atzeret is the eighth day of assembly Simchat Torah- rejoicing in the Torah

Booths. This will be the punishment of Egypt, and the punishment of all the nations who do not go up to celebrate the Feast of Booths.[53]

Shemini Atzeret שמיני עצרת

Shemini Atzeret occurs on the 22nd of Tishrei, and it is known as The Eighth Day of Assembly (Numbers 29:35). Although it is a continuation of Sukkot, it is considered a separate festival. It is a high Shabbat, so the rituals of Kiddush, candle lighting, and no work apply. On this day, the family does not eat meals in the sukkah, and the lulav and etrog are not used in the services.

One striking difference between Sukkot and Shemini Atzeret is in the number of Temple sacrifices. The previous seven days of Sukkot totaled 70 sacrifices in all (Nu 29:12-32). On Shemini Atzeret, the burnt offering consists of one ram, one bullock and seven lambs. The rabbis say the 70 sacrifices refer to the seventy nations (mankind), while the one ram and one bullock represent the special relationship between G-d and Israel.

In the synagogue, one of the specific prayers is for rain, and all recite the *yizkor*, the memorial prayer for the dead[54]. Yizkor provides a way to publically acknowledge those special people who have passed on, yet they have influenced our lives for good and for blessing.

The Talmud and Midrash explain Shemini Atzeret: "A king invited his children to a feast. After the seven days, when the departure finally arrived, the king said to his children, 'I beg of you, stay another day; it is hard to separate from you!'" (Rashi on Leviticus 23:36). The joyfulness of Sukkot is extended to Shemini Atzeret. Simchat Torah and Shemini Atzeret are celebrated on the same day in Israel, but as two days in the diaspora.

53. Zec 14:16-19 (emphasis added).

54. Suggestions for *yizkor* are included in Appendix E

Simchat Torah שמחת תורה

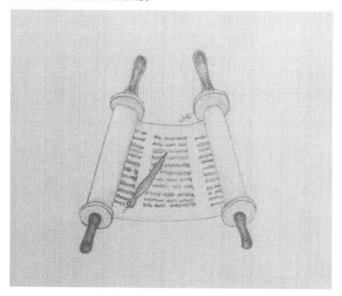

Simchat Torah means "rejoicing in the Law." The rituals of Simchat Torah revolve around the completion of the annual Torah cycle of Scripture readings and the beginning again of that same cycle.

Two men from the congregation are honored. The first is called Chatan Torah (bridegroom of the Torah). He is called to the bima[55] by a blessing, which the whole congregation speaks. The Bridegroom of the Torah will end the annual cycle of Torah readings by reading Deuteronomy 33:1-34:12.

The second man is called Chatan Bereishit (bridegroom of Bereishit[56]). He, too, is called to the bima by a blessing, which the whole congregation speaks, to begin again the cycle of Torah readings. The Bridegroom of Bereseit will read Genesis 1:1-2:3, thereby maintaining the continuity of the Torah. It has no beginning and no end, just like Yeshua, the Living Torah.

After the completion of the readings, the synagogue

55. Bima - pulpit

56. Beresheit – Hebrew name for the book of Genesis

celebrates by *hakkafot* ("circling"), walking and dancing seven circles around the bima. The Torah scrolls are removed, and the *levi'im*[57] and *kohanim*[58] are honored first to hold them. As they dance and sing around the synagogue, the scrolls are passed to others. At the end of the circuits, usually everyone has had an opportunity to hold a scroll. Those not holding scrolls are carrying small paper flags. Children are given fabric Torah Scrolls to carry and flags. It is considered a great honor to carry a scroll, and an even greater honor to lead the procession.

57. Levi'im - Levites

58. Kohanim - Priests

3

ADDITIONAL HOLIDAYS

Purim פורים

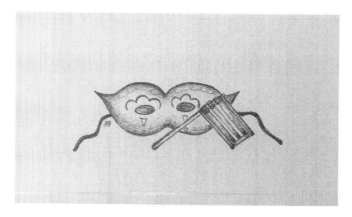

The holiday of Purim ("lots") is recorded in the book of Esther and is celebrated on the fourteenth of Adar[59]. It is named Purim because wicked Haman (may his name be blotted out) used a lot (pur) to decide when to kill the Jews. It is a celebration of Esther and Mordecai's victory over evil Haman and his plot to destroy all the Jews in the Persian Empire by manipulation of the king.

One tradition of Purim is a way of erasing Haman's name forever. While the scroll of Esther is being read

59. Adar – Hebrew month before Passover Feb-Mar

55

in the synagogue, groggers (noise makers) and loud voices drown out Haman's name each time it is read in order to keep Haman's name from being heard.

There is a festive meal on Purim; gifts of food are sent to friends (*mishloach manot*) and money to the poor (*mattanot le-evyonim*). Hamentaschen, triangular shaped pastries with a filling in the center, are usually in the Purim baskets. The name means "Hamen's pockets," presumably a reference to the money with which Haman tried to bribe King Ahasuerus to kill the Jews. The basket also may contain little bottles of wine or beer, cakes, fruit and nuts. In older times, special plates were made on which to place the gifts. *Mattanot le-evyonim* is fulfilling a *mitzvah* (commandment) to give to the poor. This mitzvah allows the less fortunate to enjoy the holiday, too.

The day is celebrated with costumes, wearing of masks, plays, parodies, and a consumption of liquor (to drown out the memory of Haman). All of these activities create a party-like atmosphere where everything becomes topsy-turvy. It is a great day of fun and celebration. In Israel there are parades and carnivals to enjoy. In the United States, many synagogues and individuals hold parties.

Purim rituals are based on Esther 9:22:

> ... because on those days the Jews
> rid themselves of their enemies, and
> it was a month which was turned
> for them from sorrow into gladness
> and from mourning into a holiday;
> that they should make them days of
> feasting and rejoicing and sending
> portions of food to one another and
> gifts to the poor.

Although the name of G-d is not mentioned in the book of Esther, HaShem's hand is apparent in all that occurs. Esther is the only book in the Bible where G-d is not specifically mentioned.

Hanukkah חנוכה

Hanukkah means "dedication." It is also called the Festival of Lights or Feast of Dedication. It begins on the 25th of Kislev[60]. This festival lasts eight days and is a celebration of the victory of the Maccabees[61] over the Greeks.

Alexander the Great, after conquering the known world, died, and his empire was divided following his death. After a time, the land of Israel came under the rule of the Seleucid dynasty, which also ruled Syria. In 167 BCE, King Antiochus Epiphanes made a decree that all of the people under his rule would be forced to Hellenize. The worship of Greek deities and the sacrifice and offering of pigs replaced the traditional worship in the Temple. Torah observances like Shabbat and circumcision were outlawed, as was Torah study.

Although there were some Jews who openly embraced the changes, there were some who rejected these laws. As punishment for their

60. Kislev-
Hebrew month
Nov-Dec

61. Maccabees
– Jewish family
that fought
against the
Greeks

57

disobedience, the *mohels* who performed the circumcisions and the circumcised infant were hung by the neck in the doorway of their homes until dead. This is but one of the horrors faced by those who tried to keep the commandments.

One day in the town of Modi'in, the Greek army set up an altar and demanded that the Jews in that area sacrifice a pig on that altar. In a show of obedience to the decrees of King Antiochus, a Jew about to follow that decree was killed by Matthias, an old priest.

Matthias and his five sons began to fight a guerrilla war against the Greek army, retreating to the mountains and enlisting the help of other Jews to fight also. Before Matthias died, he passed his mantle of leadership onto his son, Judah the Maccabee. It was Judah and his warriors that finally freed the Temple from the Greek armies.

The rabbis record a miracle that when the Temple was once again in Jewish hands, and after being cleansed from defilement, the priests found a single container of oil. This container bore the correct seal, and it was used to light the *menorah*. The menorah, once lit, burned for eight consecutive days even though the container of oil should only have lasted one day.

Many Hanukkah traditions revolve around the *menorah*, light, and oil. The candelabrum that holds nine candles is a *hanukkiah*. It holds eight candles, one for each day, and the ninth one is the *shamash* (servant) candle. After dark, the *shamash* candle is lit, and from that candle, additional candles for each night are lit until day eight, when all nine candles are lit. It is a beautiful picture of Israel's increasing light in the world.

It is interesting that the *shamash*, the servant, is the source of light for all the other candles. This is a

picture of Messiah Yeshua, who is the Light of the World. From Him mankind receives light (illumination), and Israel reflects that light to everything around us.

Some traditional foods are *latkes* (shredded potatoes) fried in oil, and *sufganiyot* (donuts). Eating foods fried in oil during this holiday is a remembrance of the oil that lasted all eight days.

The custom to give *gelt* at Hanukah is a very old one. Gelt is the Yiddish word for money. Gelt today is generally chocolate coins wrapped in gold or silver foil. The chocolate has been imprinted with symbols, usually a *menorah*, and the word Israel, as well as other words or symbols -- for example, the shekel.

Having the right to print coins in the ancient world was not only prestigious, but a concrete expression of independence or autonomy of the people or nation. That expression continues through the use of *gelt* at Hanukkah.

Another custom is to play *dreidel*. A dreidel is a small

four-sided top for spinning that has a Hebrew letter on each side: nun נ , gimmel ג , hey ה , and shin שׁ. They stand for the words *nes gadol haya sham* ("a great miracle happened **there**").

In Israel, the letter *shin* is replaced by *pey* פ (a great miracle happened **here**).

To play the game, all players must put something in the pot -- usually pennies, nuts, gelt (chocolate coins). The players then take turns spinning the dreidel and following the instructions: The letter *nun* נ means nothing; you neither put in the pot nor take out. The letter *gimmel* ג means you take the whole pot. The letter hey ה means you take out half of the pot, rounding up if uneven amounts. The letter shin שׁ means you put one in (coin, walnut, gelt), etc. Another game is to take one's spinning dreidel and see how many other spinning dreidels he or she can knock out.

There are many stories about how Jews incorporated the dreidel into the holiday traditions. One tale is that the Jews played dreidel, which allowed them to gather publicly and discuss Torah or exchange news. When the enemy soldiers went by, it looked like Jews had gathered for a game of chance. Any loud voices in discussion simply seemed a game being enjoyed.

Hanukkah was celebrated in Yeshua's day, as it reads in John 10:22-23: "At that time the Feast of the Dedication took place at Jerusalem; it was winter, and Yeshua was walking in the temple in the portico of Solomon."[62]

Hanukkah also is about the rededication of the altar from paganism and idolatry to worship again of the G-d of Israel according to His instructions. It is also a time for individuals to rededicate personal altars and look for any pagan (foreign) practices and attitudes. It is a time of recommitment to HaShem.

THE BIBLICAL AND JEWISH YEARS

The Numbering of Years

There are two cycles that can be used as the basis for a calendar. One is the solar cycle, which is based on the earth's yearly rotation around the sun. The other is the lunar cycle, which is based on the phases of the moon. A lunar month is approximately 29 ½ days long, but a calendar month must be measured in whole days. Since two lunar cycles equal 59 days, the months alternate between having 29 and 30 days.

The Hebrew calendar is based on twelve lunar months. This twelve-month lunar year is rounded up to 354 days, so there is a difference between the lunar and solar calendar by eleven days each year. In order to keep the festivals within their specified seasons, a leap year will occur. Seven times in nineteen years a thirteenth month is added; this month is named Adar II. The calendar having this additional month is called a leap year.

Compared to a modern Gregorian calendar, a Jewish calendar will have an unusual year date; for instance, the Hebrew year 5777 began on Rosh Hashanah of the Gregorian year 2016. The date 5777 is the number of years that have passed since the creation of the world. It was determined by counting back the years in the Bible. Maimonides[63] is credited with setting this date. Maimonides, who was the first to codify the Jewish Law in his book *Mishneh Torah*, acknowledged that the process of numbering the yearly calendar date by the years of the world was in use well before he compiled his book.

New Years

There are four new years within Judaism. Rosh HaShanah (1 Tishrei) and 1 Nisan are the two most prominent new years. Elul 1 is for tithing on animals, and the 15th of Shevat is considered a new year with respect to certain agricultural laws related to tithing.

1. Tishrei 1, Rosh HaShanah, is the beginning of the civil calendar, and it is traditionally the birth date of the world. In the Torah it is called Yom Teruah, the Day of Blowing, because a shofar is sounded and heard 100 times on that day.

Rosh HaShanah is the new year for measuring the reigns of foreign kings, so whether a king reigned a full year or a partial year, the first day of Tishrei served as the standard anniversary marking the end of a full

63. Moses ben Maimon, born in Spain in 1135

year of reign.

The first of Tishrei is also the new year for setting the Sabbatical (*Shemitah*) year and the Jubilee *(Yovel)* year, when applicable.

Tishrei 1 is also the new year when determining the yearly tithe (*ma'aser*), a ten percent tax on vegetables and grains. The Levites and priests were supported by these tithes because they did not own or cultivate their own land. The tithe for a particular year had to be paid with produce from that same year, thus requiring a fixed date to begin and end each fiscal year.

Tithing the produce or grain involved three processes: (1) The owner removed the first tithe (*ma'aser rishon*), and it was paid to the Levites. (2) The Levites then tithed their ten percent of that for the priests. This tithe was called *terumah*. (3) After separating the first tithe, the owner was required to set aside a second tithe (*ma'aser sheni*) from the remainder of his produce.

In the first, second, fourth, and fifth years of the sabbatical cycle, the owner was required to consume this second tithe in Jerusalem. If the distance was too great or it was too difficult for the individual to bring the actual grain, he was required to sell it and purchase food to be eaten in Jerusalem. In the third and sixth years, the owner distributed this second tithe to the poor (*ma'aser ani*).

2. Shevat 15, Tu'B'Shevat, is the new year for trees. This is the new year for designating fruits as *orlah*, that which is forbidden to be eaten during the first three years of a fruit tree's planting, for *Reva'i*, the fourth year of a fruit tree's planting where the fruit is holy to Hashem[64], and for separating fruits for tithing.

On Tu'B'Shevat, it is customary to eat for the first time a fruit from the new season, particularly one typical

64. Le 19:23-25

to be found in *Eretz Yisrael*, the Land of Israel, and to say the Shehecheyanu blessing: "Blessed are You, Adonai Eloheinu, King of the universe, who has kept us alive, sustained us, and brought us to this season."

The first humans once ate the fruit from the Tree of the Knowledge of Good and Evil in the Garden; now believers eat the good fruit from the good land, symbolizing a better choice to receive sustenance from the Tree of Life. Following the Sephardic mystics of Safed[65], many will celebrate this new year with a small Seder that utilizes the fruit as a symbol of humans as it says in Deuteronomy 20:19 "...for is the tree of the field a man...?"

Just as in the Passover Seder, on Tu B'Shevat, participants drink four cups of wine. Eating fruit with large pits represents the giant accomplishments achieved by those who have gone before, like Moses. Eating some fruit with small seeds represents the small, everyday actions each person does to create a better world. In this better world, one performs those acts of kindness without expectation of reward or recognition. One focuses on opening himself to HaShem's holiness, a willingness to change and transform, and to tell others about Him.

Illusion and deception entered the world when Adam and Eve ate the fruit from the Tree of the Knowledge of Good and Evil in the Garden. Things are not so clear cut as before the fall, so on this day, Israel chooses to plant seeds of hope and truth and to ask for deception and illusion to be eradicated. For believers in Messiah Yeshua, it is a way of embracing our destiny to be conformed into the image of Messiah.

In Israel today, this new year has come to symbolize the redemption of the land and the need for environmental awareness. It is celebrated nationwide with tree planting, i.e., Arbor Day.

65. Safed – Town in Northern Israel spelled several ways: Tsefat, Zefat, Sefat. Rabbi Isaac Luria lived and taught there.

3. Nisan 1, the third new year, corresponds to the season of redemption from Egypt and the beginning of the Nation of Israel. This is the beginning of the religious year. The Torah reads: "This month shall be the beginning of months for you; it is to be the first month of the year to you."[66] This month is so significant that all the moedim are counted starting from this date.

The first day of Nisan is the new year for measuring the reign of Jewish kings (notice not the foreign ones), for the renting of houses, and for the counting involved in the prohibition against delaying the fulfillment of vows. When an individual chooses an object or animal he desires to dedicate to the Sanctuary, he must fulfill that vow before three festivals have passed (starting with Passover).

The first day of Nisan is also the due date for using the half-shekel contribution to purchase the communal sacrifices for the Temple described in Shabbat Shekalim. Those half-shekels were required by all males over the age of 20. The rich could not give more and the poor could not give less, thereby rendering all men equal.

The half-shekel tax was due on the fifteenth day of Adar, and tables for collection were placed in the provinces. By the 25th of Adar, tables were set up in the Temple to collect the tax. If an individual chose to pay the tax in Jerusalem at the Temple, he would find there shofar-chests. One was inscribed "new shekel," which was the tax for that year, and the other "old shekel," where the tax, if not collected from the previous year, could still be paid.

In later years, the Temple tax would not only be used for communal sacrifices but also for Temple repair, road maintenance, and white washing tombs in order for everything to be ready for the worshipper to go up to Jerusalem to celebrate the three pilgrimage festivals: Unleavened Bread, Shavuot and Sukkot.

66. Ex 12:2

At these three moedim, the Torah required all males to go up to Jerusalem; always when the Scripture records "go up," it is not just a natural ascension, but most definitely a spiritual one. Hence, worshipers "go up to Jerusalem," the spiritual city of the Great King.

4. Elul 1 is the new year for tithing cattle. The tithe for cattle had to be made from cattle born in the same fiscal year, between the first day of Elul and the next fiscal year.

5

FAST DAYS

There are seven fast days, and they are divided into major and minor fast days.

There are four fast days associated with the destruction of the Temple, the city of Jerusalem, and the loss of the independent state of ancient Israel. Zechariah 8:19 refers to these as "…the fast of the fourth, the fast of the fifth, the fast of the seventh, and the fast of the tenth months will become joy, gladness, and cheerful feasts for the house of Judah; so love truth and peace." As the counting (of the months) begins with the month of Nisan, Zechariah refers respectively to the 17th of Tammuz (fourth month); the 9th of Av (the fifth month); the Fast of Gedaliah[67], the 3rd of Tishrei (seventh month); and the 10th of Tevet (tenth month).

Since the establishment of the state of Israel, there are Jews who question the continual observance of these fast days commemorating the destruction of the Temple and loss of self-rule. Traditionalists maintain that Israel should continue to fast since the Temple has not been rebuilt, Messiah has not come, and complete redemption is not fully realized in the earth.

67. Fast of Gedaliah – commemorates the assassination of Gedaliah ben Achikam, a Jew who was selected by King Nebuchadnezzar to be governor of Israel following the destruction of the First Temple. His assassination ended any hope of self-rule in Israel.

MAJOR FAST DAYS

Major fast days are Yom Kippur (Day of Atonement) and Tisha B'Av (Ninth of Av).

1. Tisha B'Av commemorates the destruction of both Temples. Both the First and Second Temple fell on that date. The First Temple was destroyed by the Babylonians in 586 BCE, and the Second Temple by the Romans in 70 CE. Many other tragedies the Jewish people suffered also happened on this date; for example, the Jews were expelled from England in 1290 CE and from Spain in 1492 CE.

Tisha B'Av is the culmination of a three-week period of mourning that begins on the seventeenth of Tammuz. On this date in history, King Nebuchadnezzar of Babylon breached the walls of Jerusalem following a long siege during which the inhabitants of Jerusalem were ravaged by hunger and epidemics. On the seventh of Av he began to destroy Jerusalem, and by the tenth of Av, the Temple was destroyed and Jerusalem was ravished. It is tradition during this three-week mourning period to refrain from parties, weddings, cutting hair, etc.; refraining from these activities are all signs of mourning.

The restrictions on Tisha B'Av are similar to Yom Kippur: Jews do not eat or drink, (not even water), bathe, shave, wear cosmetics or leather shoes. Couples do not engage in marital intimacy from sundown the evening before until sundown of this day. Women who are pregnant or people who are ill do not need to fast.

In the synagogue, the book of *Eicha* (Lamentations) is read and mourning prayers are recited. The Ark (the cabinet which holds the Torah scroll and additional scrolls) is draped in black.

If the Ninth of Av falls on a Shabbat, the fast is postponed until the next day.

2. Yom Kippur, the Day of Atonement, falls on the tenth of Tishrei. The significance of this day is discussed in the chapter Seven Moedim. The fast begins from sundown the evening before and ends after sundown on this day. The fast is between 24 to 27 hours long, for some continue to fast until the stars are visible in the sky.

Jews do not eat or drink (not even water), bathe, shave, or wear cosmetics or leather shoes. Couples do not engage in marital intimacy. Individuals who are ill do not need to fast. It is a personal decision for pregnant women to make. They are permitted to decide whether they fast or not.

MINOR FAST DAYS

There are five minor fast days: Ta'anit Esther, Ta'anit Bechorim, Asarah B'Tevet, Tzom Tamuz, Tzom Gedaliah. The words ta'anit (תענית) and tzom (צום) both mean fast.

1. Ta'anit Esther the Fast of Esther. This fast is from sunrise until sunset on Purim eve, commemorating the three-day fast observed by the Jewish people in the story of Purim found in the book of Esther. If the date of the Fast of Esther falls on Shabbat (Saturday), the fast is instead observed on the preceding Thursday.

2. Ta'anit Bechorim the Fast of the Firstborn. This fast is in commemoration of the firstborn being spared during the last plague of the Exodus. This fast is not as widely observed as it once was. This fast also applies to the firstborn son following a miscarriage. The fast begins at sunrise and ends at sunset before Pesach (fourteenth of Nisan).

3. Asarah B'Tevet the tenth of Tevet. This fast occurs closely after Hanukkah. It is one of the four fast days that commemorates the destruction of one or both of the Temples. This fast is observed from sunrise to sunset and commemorates the siege on Jerusalem by King Nebuchadnezzar and the Babylonians. This siege led to the destruction of the First Temple.

4. Tzom Tamuz the Fast of the seventeenth of Tamuz. This fast is from sunrise to sunset and commemorates the breaching of the walls of Jerusalem by Nebuchadnezzar's army.

5. Tzom Gedaliah the Fast of Gedaliah, is observed on the third of Tishrei and is kept from sunrise until sunset. It commemorates the assassination of Gedaliah ben Achicam, the first Jewish governor appointed by the Babylonians after the First Temple was destroyed. The Jews who had fled from the Babylonians into the surrounding lands of Ammon, Moab, and Edom heard of Gedaliah's appointment and returned to Judah. Under his excellent leadership, these Jews cultivated the ground, and once again the Land responded with bountiful harvests.

Unfortunately, a man named Ishmael ben Netaniah was jealous of Gedaliah's position and unhappy with his Babylonian alliance. He and ten men joined Gedaliah to celebrate Rosh Hashanah. Their feast days ended with the murder not only of Gedaliah but with the other Jews and the Babylonian soldiers present. More fighting ensued, and the Jews fled into Egypt, ending all prospects of Jewish settlements in Judea. The actions of Ishmael and his men thus made the Babylonian exile absolute. This story is recorded in Jeremiah chapters 40-43, and an abbreviated version is in II Kings 25.

MODERN HOLIDAYS AND REMEMBRANCES

Four new holidays have been added to the Jewish calendar since the establishment of the State of Israel. They are Yom HaShoah (Holocaust Remembrance Day), Yom HaZikaron (Memorial Day), Yom HaAtzma'ut (Independence Day), and Yom Yerushalayim (Jerusalem Day). They are national holidays in Israel.

Yom HaShoah: Holocaust Remembrance Day
יום השואה

This day falls on the twenty-seventh of Nisan. It was established by the Israeli government to commemorate the Holocaust and its victims. It is not clear why this particular date was chosen. One opinion is that the anniversary of the Warsaw Ghetto uprising during WWII, which began before Pesach concluded on April 27, 1943, (although active fighting continued for a week or more). Jews who were housed in the ghetto there led an armed resistance against the German soldiers who had arrived to deport the rest of the Jews to the concentration camps. The Jews were successful in holding off the German troops for about three weeks before they were overcome and deported. This resistance against the Germans instilled hope and mobilized others within European ghettos to resist.

In Israel today Yom HaShoah is marked by a siren sounding for two minutes of silence at sunset the evening before and at 11:00 a.m. on the designated day. Literally, pedestrians and traffic will stop and observe the two minutes of silence no matter where they are or what they are doing. The rituals for this day are still being developed; the day is also observed by the closing of banks, schools, theatres and most businesses.

In the United States, there are many and varied programs held at synagogues and in communities; survivors speak and testify to their experiences. It is a time to honor those who are living and to remember those who have perished during the Holocaust.

Yom HaZikaron: Memorial Day יום הזכרון

This day always falls on the day before Yom HaAtzma'ut, Israeli Independence Day, as established by the Knesset. On this day Israel remembers the soldiers who lost their lives fighting the War of Independence and in other combat situations. The War of Independence, also known as the Arab-Israeli War, began on May 15, 1948, one day after the creation of the State of Israel. The armies from the five Arab nations of Syria, Egypt, Saudi Arabia, Lebanon, and Jordan invaded Israel. Although the Arab armies were better trained and supplied, the Israelis fought back successfully. The war was characterized by long periods of fighting and times of cease-fire. The war ended in January 1949.

Yom HaAtzma'ut: Israeli Independence Day
יום העצמאות

This day marks the establishment of the modern State of Israel on May 14, 1948. It normally is observed on the 5th of Iyar unless the date for Yom HaZikaron (Memorial Day for fallen soldiers) would fall on Shabbat. In that case, the date would be moved to either just before or after the 5th of Iyar. This occurs because the custom is not to fast or be solemn and sad on Shabbat. Since Yom HaZikaron is a solemn day, it will not be celebrated on a Shabbat. Clearly there would be no Independence Day without the sacrifice of the soldiers. It is a national holiday, so almost everyone is off work. There are public ceremonies and some families will enjoy the day by hiking, picnicking, or touring an Army camp.

Yom Yerushalayim: Jerusalem Day יום ירושלים

Jerusalem Day falls on the 28th of Iyar. It is the anniversary of the date of the liberation of the Old City of Jerusalem and unification of all of Jerusalem during the Six-Day War. It is generally only observed in Israel.

The Six-Day War started on June 5, 1967 (27th of Iyar), when Arab countries attacked Israel again. Although Jerusalem was not under attack at the beginning, Jordan sent soldiers into Jerusalem and suddenly the city of Jerusalem became the focus of the war. Again HaShem delivered His people and His city. This was the first time in 2,000 years since the destruction of the Temple in 70CE that a foreign power was not in control of Jerusalem.

The Chief Rabbi of Israel ruled that each year on the 28th of Iyar, the Hallel[68] will be recited with the blessing (below), for the liberation of Jerusalem carries with it the hope that the prophetic vision of Jerusalem shall soon be realized. This is the sacred vision of world peace and the desire to know the paths of the G-d of Israel expressed in the words of Isaiah 2:1-5:

> The mountain of the House of the Lord shall be established…and all the nations shall flow to it, and many people shall come and say: 'Let us go to the mountain of the Lord… that He may teach us His ways…' For out of Zion shall go forth the Torah, and the word of the Lord from Jerusalem….and they shall beat their swords into plowshares, and their

68. Hallel – literally praise, Psalms 113-118

spears into pruning hooks; nation
shall not lift up sword against nation,
neither shall they learn war any
more.

Special prayers and readings are said in synagogues
around the world. In Israel, ceremonies are held at the
Kotel (Western Wall of the Temple) and Ammunition
Hill.   Ammunition Hill was a former Jordanian military
outpost. It experienced the heaviest fighting during
the Six Day War.   It is now a national memorial site.

7

ADDITIONAL INFORMATION

Candle Lighting Times

Many calendars contain candle lighting times for major cities. Locate the city closest to you to know when to light Shabbat candles. It is customary to light the Shabbat candles eighteen minutes prior to sunset, so the times on a Jewish calendar reflect that. If one is too late and missed lighting candles prior to sundown, do NOT light candles. Israel is commanded _not_ to kindle a light on Shabbat.

Chol HaMoed חול המועד

"The weekday of the festival" refers to the weekdays (non-holy days), the intermediate days of Passover and Sukkot. There are certain Biblical passages that are read on these days, but there are no restrictions like Shabbat.

Counting the Omer

The days between Passover and Shavuot are counted off for 50 days. This is called "Counting the Omer." The count starts the second night of Passover and ends the evening before Shavuot:

> You shall also count for yourselves
> from the day after the Sabbath,
> from the day when you brought in
> the sheaf of the wave offering; there
> shall be seven complete Sabbaths.
> 'You shall count fifty days to the day
> after the seventh Sabbath; then you
> shall present a new grain offering to
> the L-rd.' [69]

There is a blessing each night:

> Blessed are you, HaShem, Our G-d, King of
> the universe, Who has sanctified us with His
> commandments and has commanded us
> regarding the counting of the Omer. Today
> is <u>one</u> day of the Omer.

Once day seven is reached, the blessing is:

> Blessed are you, HaShem,
> Our G-d, King of the universe,
> Who has sanctified us with
> His commandments and has
> commanded us regarding the
> counting of the Omer. Today is
> seven days, which is one week of the
> Omer.

The days after follow this pattern:

> ...Today is eight days, which are one
> week and one day of the Omer.

> ...Today is eighteen days, which
> are two weeks and four days, of the
> Omer."

Counting is part of the spiritual preparation to receive the gift of the Torah at Mount Sinai. Each year,

69. Le 23:15-16

anticipate deeper revelation as preparation for this festival. It is not enough to just be free of Egypt; one needs to be transformed into part of a Holy Nation. As part of the counting, some congregations read portions of selected Psalms and meditate on them to prepare the heart.

Lag'b'Omer ל״ג בעומר

Lag'b'Omer is the 33rd day of the counting of the Omer; the numerical value of the Hebrew letters ל lamed (30) and ג gimel (3) is 33; hence, "lag, the thirty-third day."

In times past, the counting of the Omer was always associated with solemnity and mourning. The rabbis have varying opinions on this, but many agree the mourning was lifted on the thirty-third day. The custom became to hold picnics, weddings, and cut hair on that date (all things that would have been prohibited during mourning).

Rosh Chodesh ראש חדש

The "head of the month," is often translated as "new moon." In Judaism, the calendar is a lunar one based on the cycles of the moon:

> Then Elohim said, 'Let there be lights
> in the expanse of the heavens to
> separate the day from the night,
> and let them be for signs, and for
> seasons, and for days and years.' [70]

> Now HaShem said to Moses and
> Aaron in the land of Egypt, 'This
> month shall be the head of months
> for you; it is to be the first month of
> the year to you.' [71]

David, who had been anointed as the future king, observed the new moon in King Saul's court:

70. Ge 1:14

71. Ex 12:1-2

So David said to Jonathan, 'Behold, tomorrow is the new moon, and I ought to sit down to eat with the king. But let me go, that I may hide myself in the field until the third evening.' [72]

In ancient Israel, it was customary to inquire of a prophet on the new moon, which is documented in the Shunammite woman's visit:

And he said, 'Why will you go to him today? It is neither new moon nor Sabbath.' And she said, 'It will be well.' [73]

Ancient Israel blew the shofar over new moon offerings and blessed HaShem:

Blow the trumpet at the new moon, at the full moon, on our feast day. For it is a statute for Israel, An ordinance of the G-d of Jacob.[74]

Also in the day of your gladness and in your appointed feasts, and on the first days of your months, you shall blow the trumpets over your burnt offerings and over the sacrifices of your peace offerings; and they shall be as a reminder of you before your G-d. I am the L-rd your G-d.[75]

72. I Sa 20:5

73. 2 Ki 4:23

74. Ps 81:3-4

75. Nu 10:10

76. For more ideas on activities to commemorate and learn more about the new moon, see K. Gallagher's BEKY Book, *The Biblical New Moon: A Beginner's Guide for Celebrating.*

Today Jews still gather as it is commanded, say blessings, sing songs, and talk about the significance of the new month. The sages considered the new moon a mini Yom Kippur, a time to start over with a fresh slate and renew one's self in service to the King. [76]

Shekels

The Biblical commandment to give the Holy Half

Shekel may once again be observed. The holy half shekel can be purchased and given through www. begedivri.com.

Tu' B'Av

Tu B'Av is the 15ᵗʰ of the month of Av. It is a Chag Ahava, a day of love. Tu'B'Av was observed in ancient Israel as a matchmaking day for unmarried women when the virgin daughters would wear white and dance in the vineyards. In Judges 21, the men from other tribes placed a vow on themselves that they would not allow their daughters to marry into the tribe of Benjamin. However, in their compassion they devised a way to circumvent their vow. In modern Israel, and among many Jewish people, the day is celebrated similar to Valentine's Day, a celebration of love.

CONCLUSION

Shabbat and the festival days provide holiness, rhythm, and harmony to our lives as we observe them. It makes sense that if the CEO of the universe has called the meeting that we would gladly appear before Him at His set time.

Shabbat is a weekly reminder of HaShem's great love for us, for He provided a day of rest and refreshment. Shabbat is not a day to laze around and do nothing or chase after our own desires, but rather it is an opportunity to ascend spiritually as we study the Word and commune with the Creator.

The ancient Jewish sages have set an orderly way for Israel to read the entire Torah each year; there are additional readings to emphasize those special Sabbaths.

A believer in Yeshua who understands the Jewish calendar can participate fully in the feasts of G-d and His people, His weekly Shabbat, the fasts and commemorative holidays. The mystery now removed, each individual may embrace the spiritual journey toward deep and lasting transformation, a journey of increasing holiness that is renewed each year.

QUESTIONS FOR REVIEW

1. Contemplate your own weekly Sabbath observance. How can you make it more meaningful for yourself, your family?

2. The Haftorah for Parsha Mishapatim (ordinances) (Exodus 30:11-16) is usually Jeremiah 34:8-22, 33:25-26. When Parsha Mishpatim occurs on Shabbat Shekalim that reading is replaced with II Kings 11:17-12:17.

Read Mishpatim and both haftorah readings. How are the rabbis using these readings to coincide and teach the Parsha for that week?

3. Reviewing the fall moedim, how are the themes of repentance, kingship, judgment and atonement reflected in the readings, liturgy, and rituals?

4. What is the thirty-third day of Counting the Omer referred to? What is special about it?

5. Considering how the rabbis view Rosh Chodesh as a mini Yom Kippur, how would that be reflected in your own observance of the day?

6. During Hanukkah we eat latkes and donuts, play dreidel with gelt, and light an additional candle each night. What do these specific items teach about the holiday? What spiritual principles are imparted by incorporating them?

7. By performing the ritual of *bedikat chametz* prior to Pesach what are we learning and teaching?

8. Using the elements of the Passover Seder, compare and contrast the "L-rd's Supper" found in the Brit Chadasha. Note when the wine is drunk, etc…

9. At Rosh HaShanah we are to "hear" the shofar, not necessarily be the one to blow it. Identify the sounds being blown and their purposes. Compare this to
I Corinthians 14: 7-8.

10. Sukkot is known as the "season of our rejoicing." It follows after all of the harvest is brought in. How can this connect to Yeshua's birth and the final ingathering of all exiles to the G-d of Abraham, Isaac, and Jacob?

APPENDIX A

Challah Recipe
Shabbat

Ingredients:

- 7/8 cup water
- 3 egg yolks
- 3 cups bread flour
- 1 ½ teaspoon salt
- ¼ cup butter or oil
- 3/8 cup sugar
- 2 teaspoons active dry yeast or 1 packet Fleischman's Rapid Rise
- 1 egg, beaten

Directions:

Place the first seven ingredients in a bread machine pan. Select the Dough setting and press Start. When the dough is ready, turn it onto a floured board. Turn on your oven for two minutes at 250 degrees, and then TURN IT OFF.

Divide the dough into four equal pieces. Shape each one into a long, thin braid no longer than the length of the baking sheet. Transfer them to a greased baking sheet, placing them parallel.

Pinch one end of all four pieces together at one end and begin braiding them under and over (see YouTube for step-by-step visual instructions or creative holiday braids).

When the whole loaf is braided, tuck under both ends to make it neat.

Paint the loaf with the beaten egg and allow to rise in the warmed oven for 30-45 minutes. Sprinkle with poppy or sesame seeds. Bake at 350 degrees for 25-35 minutes until the top is a deep, rich brown.

GLUTEN FREE CHALLAH

Gluten-free challah recipes often will mix like a batter instead of a dough, so if you're interested in a traditional look, silicone molds are available, such as The Kosher Cook KCBW0160 Royal Challah Silicone Baking pan.

Ingredients:

- 2 cups rice flour
- 1¾ cups tapioca flour
- ¼ cup sugar
- 2 teaspoons sugar
- 3 teaspoons xanthan gum
- ½ teaspoon salt
- ⅔ cup lukewarm water
- 1 cup lukewarm water
- 1½ tablespoons yeast
- 4 tablespoons melted butter
- 1 teaspoon apple cider vinegar
- 4 eggs
- sesame seed (optional)

Directions:

In mixer, combine the flours, 1/4 c sugar, xantham gum, and salt.

Dissolve the 2 tsp sugar in the 2/3 cup of water and mix in the yeast. In a separate bowl combine the butter with the additional 1 cup water and vinegar.

With mixer on low speed, blend the dry ingredients. Slowly add the butter/water mixture. Blend in the eggs, 1 at a time. The dough should feel slightly warm. Pour the yeast mixture into the ingredients in the bowl and beat the highest speed for 2 minutes.

Place the bowl in a warm spot, cover with greased plastic wrap and a towel, and let rise approximately 1 hour.

Return the dough to the mixer and beat on high for 3 minutes. Spoon the dough into a greased, floured loaf pan. Fill 2/3 full, you may bake the remainder in greased muffin tins. Sprinkle tops with sesame seeds. Let the dough rise until it is slightly above the tops of the pans, about 45-60 minutes.

Preheat the oven to 400 F and bake the loaf for approximately 1 hour.

APPENDIX B

Parashiot: Torah and Haftorah
Special Shabbatot

PARASHIOT FROM THE TORAH, HAFTARAH AND BRIT CHADASHAH
] Bracket Indicates Double Reading

B'REISHEET	*in the beginning*	Gen. 1:1-6:8, Is. 42:5-43:10, Rev 22:6-21
Noach	*Noah (rest)*	Gen. 6:9-11:32, Is. 54:1-55:5, Mat 24:36-46
Lech L'Cha	*go forth, yourself!*	Gen. 12:1-17:27, Is. 40:27-41:16, Rom. 4:1-25
Vayera	*and He appeared*	Gen. 18:1-22:24, 2 Ki. 4:1-37, Lk. 1:26-38; 24:26-53
Chayei Sarah	*life of Sarah*	Gen. 23:1-25:18, 1 Ki. 1:1-31, Mt. 1:1-17
Tol'dot	*generations*	Gen. 25:19-28:9, Mal. 1:1-2:7, Rom. 9:1-13
Vayetse	*and he went out*	Gen. 28:10-32:2, Hos. 11:7-14:9, John 1:19-51
Vayishlach	*and he sent*	Gen. 32:3-36:43, Obad. 1:1-21, Heb. 11:11-20
Vayeshev	*and he settled*	Gen. 37:1-40:23, Amos 2:6-3:8, Mt. 1:1-6, 16-25
Miketz	*at the end of*	Gen. 41:1-44:17, 1 Ki. 3:15-4:1, Mt. 27:15-46
Vayigash	*and he drew near*	Gen. 44:18-47:27, Ezek. 37:15-28, Lk. 6:12-16
Vay'chi	*and he lived*	Gen. 47:28-50:26, 1 Ki. 2:1-12, 1 Pet. 1:1-9
SH'MOT	*names*	Ex. 1:1-6:1, Is. 27:6-28:13, 29:22-23, Acts 7:17-35, 1 Cor. 14:13-25
Va'Era	*and I appeared*	Ex. 6:2-9:35, Ezek. 28:25-29:21, Rev. 16:1-21
Bo	*enter!*	Ex. 10:1-13:16, Jer. 46:13-28, Rom. 9:14-29
B'Shalach	*when he let go*	Ex. 13:17-17:16, Jud. 4:4-5:31, Rev. 19:1-20:6
Yitro	*Jethro (abundance)*	Ex. 18:1-20:26, Isa. 6:1-7:6, 9:5-6, Mt. 5:8-20
Mishpatim	*judgments*	Ex. 21:1-24:18, Jer. 34:8-22; 33:25-26, Mt. 5:38-42, 17:1-11
T'rumah	*offering*	Ex. 25:1-27:19, 1 Ki. 5:12-6:13, 2 Cor. 9:1-15, Mt. 5:33-37
T'tsaveh	*you shall command*	Ex. 27:20-30:10, Ezek. 43:10-27, Heb. 13:10-16
Ki Tisa	*when you elevate*	Ex. 30:11-34:35, 1 Ki. 18:1-39, 2 Cor. 3:1-18
VaYakhel ⌐	*and he assembled*	Ex. 35:1-38:20, 1 Ki. 7:13-26, Heb. 9:1-11, 1 Cor. 3:11-18
P'Kudei ⌐	*accountings of*	Ex. 38:21-40:38, 1 Ki. 7:51-8:21, Heb. 8:1-12
VAYIKRA	*and he called*	Lev. 1:1-6:7, Isa. 43:21-44:23, Heb. 10:1-18
Tsav	*command!*	Lev. 6:8-8:36, Jer. 7:21-8:3; 9:22-23, Heb. 9:11-28
Sh'mini	*eighth*	Lev. 9:1-11:47, 2 Sam 6:1-7:17, Heb. 7:1-19, 8:1-6
Tazria ⌐	*she bears seed*	Lev. 12:1-13:59, 2 Ki. 4:42-5:19, John 6:8-13, Mt. 8:1-4
M'tsora ⌐	*infected one*	Lev. 14:1-15:33, 2 Ki. 7:3-20, Mt. 8:1-17
Acharei Mot ⌐	*after the death*	Lev. 16:1-18:30, Ezek. 22:1-22:19, Heb. 9:11-28
K'doshim ⌐	*holy ones*	Lev. 19:1-20:27, Amos 9:7-15, 1 Cor. 6:9-20, 1 Pet. 1:13-16
Emor	*say!*	Lev. 21:1-24:23, Ezek. 44:15-31, Lk. 14:12-24
B'Har ⌐	*on the Mount*	Lev. 25:1-26:2, Jer. 32:6-27, Lk. 4:16-21
B'Chukotai ⌐	*in My statutes*	Lev. 26:3-27:34, Jer. 16:19-17:14, Mt. 22:1-14, 2 Cor. 6:14-18

B'MIDBAR	in the wilderness	Num. 1:1-4:20, Hos. 1:10-2:20, Rom. 9:22-33
Naso	elevate!	Num. 4:21-7:89, Jud. 13:2-25, John 12:20-36
B'Ha'alot'cha	in your making go up	Num. 8:1-12:16, Zech. 2:10-4:7, Rev. 11:1-19
Sh'lach l'cha	send for yourself!	Num. 13:1-15:41, Josh. 2:1-24, Heb. 3:7-4:1
Korach	Korah	Num. 16:1-18:32, 1 Sam. 11:14-12:22, Rom. 13:1-7
Chukat⌉	Ordinance of	Num. 19:1-22:1, Jud. 11:1-33, Heb. 9:11-28, John 3:10-21
Balak⌋	Balak	Num. 22:2-25:9, Mic. 5:6-6:8, Rom. 11:25-32
Pinchas	Phinehas	Num. 25:10-29:40, 1 Ki. 18:46-19:21, John 2:13-25
Matot⌉	tribes	Num. 30:1-32:42, Jer. 1:1-2:3, Mat. 5:33-37
Mas'ei⌋	journeys	Num. 33:1-36:13, Jer. 2:4-28, 3:4, Jas. 4:1-12
D'VARIM	words	Dt. 1:1-3:22, Isa. 1:1-27, Acts 7:51-8:4, 1 Tim 3:1-7
Va'et'chanan	and I pleaded	Dt. 3:23-7:11, Isa. 40:1-26, Mt. 23:31-39, Mk. 12:28-34
Ekev	as a result	Dt. 7:12-11:25, Isa. 49:14-51:3, Heb. 11:8-13, Rom. 8:31-39
R'eh	see!	Dt. 11:26-16:17, Isa. 54:11-55:5, John 7:37-52, 1 Jn 4:1-6
Shof'tim	judges	Dt. 16:18-21:9, Isa. 51:12-52:12, John 1:19-27, Acts 3:22-23
Ki Tetse	when you go out	Dt. 21:10-25:19, Isa. 54:1-10, Mt. 5:27-30, 1 Cor. 5:1-5
Ki Tavo	when you enter in	Dt. 26:1-29:9, Isa. 60:1-60:22, Eph. 1:3-6, Rev. 21:10-27
Nitsavim⌉	you are standing	Dt. 29:10-30:20, Isa. 61:10-63:9, Rom. 10:1-12
VaYelech⌋	and he went	Dt. 31:1-30, Mic. 7:18-20, Rom. 10:1-17
Ha'azinu	give ear!	Dt. 32:1-52, 2 Sam. 22:1-51, Rom. 10:14-11:12
V'zot Hab'rachah	and this the blessing	Dt. 33:1-34:12, Josh. 1:1-18, Rev. 21:9-22:5

APPENDIX C

Concise Chart of Hebrew Months

Month Number	Hebrew Name	English Approximation	Holiday or Fast
7	Tishrei	September-October	Rosh Hashanah, Yom Kippur, Sukkot, Shemini Atzeret, Simchat Torah
8	Cheshvan	October-November	
9	Kislev	November-December	Hanukkah
10	Tevet	December-January	Fast of Tevet 10
11	Shevat	January-February	Tu B'Shvat
12	Adar I and II	February – March	Purim
1	Nissan	March-April	Passover
2	Iyar	April-May	Yom Ha'Atzmaut (Israel's Independent Day), Lag B'Omer, Yom Yerushalayim (Jerusalem Day)
3	Sivan	May-June	Shavuot
4	Tammuz	June-July	Fast of Tammuz
5	Av	July-August	Fast of Av 10
6	Elul	August-September	*see Tishrei

APPENDIX D

**Passover Basic
Charoset**

Ingredients:

- 2 apples
- ½ cup walnuts
- 2 teaspoons cinnamon
- 2 tablespoons honey
- 2 tablespoons sweet red wine or grape juice

Directions:

Makes 1 ½ cups.

Peel, core, and cut apples into chunks. Place in a food processor, add walnuts, and chop coarsely.

Add cinnamon, honey, and wine. Pulse 3-4 times to mix. Charoset should be moist, but stiff. Add a little more wine if needed. Serve at room temperature.

*Depending on fruits and nuts available in your region, experiment with different ingredients. Even varying the types of apples can create different flavors.

APPENDIX E

Yizkor Prayer

The following Yizkor prayer is printed with the gracious permission of Jeremiah Greenberg from his *Messianic Machzor*. Many of the blessings and prayers mentioned in this booklet may be located at www.messianicliturgy.com.

Our God and God of our fathers. Since ancient times You have called us to times of memorial, times of remembrance. Yom Hakippurim is one of the seasons of memorial that You gave us in Your word. We are called to remember Your great works, Your mighty salvations. We are called to remember that only in living by faith, trusting You in all things, can You be pleased. And, we are asked to do it without murmuring, the sin which caused our ancestors to miss entering the promised land.

As we trust in You now, knowing that all things work together for good to those who love You and who are called according to Your purpose, we have peace as we remember our loved ones who have passed on before us. We remember the good that they did, and what we learned from them. May the memory of those whom we recall this day influence our lives for good, and lead our thoughts away from the vain and the fleeting to that which is eternal. As we remember their virtues, let us be motivated to devote ourselves to the Great Commission, and to live holy lives that are pleasing to You. In this way, the memory of them will continue to bring forth much fruit.

We know that we cannot change the past. But teach us how to live godly lives *now*, through the power of the Holy Spirit. Help us to live wisely and unselfishly, courageously and fruitfully, in truth and understanding, in love and peace, so that those who come after us may remember us for good, as we affectionately remember those who came before us.

Lord, we now honor those of our parents who have gone on before us, thinking of the positive and the good that we had in our relationship with them. We remember others also, relatives and friends who influenced our lives for good, and who are now partaking of their eternal reward. As we take a moment now to remember these individuals, those of us whose parents are still with us can be especially thankful to You, and think of ways they might be able to honor and bless their parents.

At this time, we take a moment to honor the memories of those who nurtured us spiritually and physically. We remember the good legacy that they left to us.

Life has meaning, life has plan and purpose. Man was not created only to perish, but to have his life, and to have it more abundantly. You made us, Lord, a little lower than Yourself, and you crowned us with glory and honor. We thank You Lord for the great salvation you have given us in Messiah Yeshua. Halleluya! You are worthy of praise and adoration!! Halleluya! You've given us the victory over death! Halleluya!

APPENDIX F

**Purim
Hamentaschen Recipes**

EASY HAMENTASCHEN

Ingredients:

- 1 box cake mix (I like Duncan Hines deluxe yellow)
- 1 cup flour
- 2 eggs
- 2 Tablespoons water
- Solo™ Cake and Pastry Filling (or other thick jam, chocolate pieces, etc.)

Directions:

Combine cookie ingredients
Roll dough 1/8" thick
Cut into 3" circles
Place 1 teaspoon of filling in center
Fold in dough on three sides and pinch to make triangles
Bake at 375° for 6-8 minutes

GLUTEN-FREE HAMENTASCHEN

Ingredients:

- 11 oz Prunes (dried plums), pitted and chopped, or other similar dried fruit such as apricots
- 1 cup Raisins
- 3/4 cup Water
- 1/3 cup Lemon Juice
- 2 cup Blanched Almond Flour[77]
- 1 cup Arrowroot Flour, plus 1/2 cup for
- dusting
- 1 tsp Salt
- 1 tsp Pure Vanilla Extract
- 1/2 cup Pure Maple Syrup, + 1 Tbsp to add to the filling
- 1/4 cup Organic Coconut Oil, melted

Directions:

In a medium sized sauce pan, add the prunes, raisins, water, lemon juice, and maple syrup. Heat over medium heat.

Bring filling to a boil, while stirring. Continue to stir frequently, while "mashing" the filling with a wood spoon.

Once the liquid has reduced, and you have a thick filling of plump prunes and raisins, remove from heat and set aside for filling the cookies.

Preheat oven to 350 degrees.

In a large mixing bowl, stir together the almond flour, arrowroot, and salt.

77. Honeywell Brand™ almond flour is the lightest flour and excellent for gluten-free baking.

Add in the vanilla extract, maple syrup, and melted coconut oil. Stir until all ingredients are combined and you have a ball of cookie dough. You can use your hands for this.

Place ball of dough on to a sheet of parchment paper, adding additional arrowroot flour and kneading the dough until it is firm enough to be rolled and cut into shapes.

Place another sheet of parchment paper over the dough, and roll into a ¼" thick layer. Dust dough with additional arrowroot, as well as dip the cookie cutter in arrowroot flour, so the dough does not stick. Carefully cut circles in the dough, and remove the excess dough from around the circles.

Add about a teaspoon of filling to the center of the cookies, and carefully fold three sides in, making a triangular shape. Pinch the corners in to seal the cookies.

Transfer the parchment to a baking sheet, and bake cookies for 20 minutes. Remove from oven and place on a cooling rack.

Repeat this process using a fresh sheet of parchment, for the remainder of the dough, until you have used all of the cookie dough. Any remaining filling can be frozen and saved for future use.

APPENDIX G

Hanukkah
Latkes Recipe

Ingredients:

- 2 pounds Idaho potatoes
- 1 onion
- 2 eggs
- ¼ cup matzo meal or all-purpose flour
- Salt and freshly ground black and white pepper to taste
- Garlic salt to taste
- Vegetable oil for frying

Directions:

Grate or finely shred potatoes alternately with the onion, either by hand or using a food processor; try to shred uniformly.

Drain potatoes and onions.

Mix in eggs, then matzo meal or flour. Season with seasonings to taste.

Pour oil into a heavy skillet or deep fryer and heat. For a skillet, pour to a depth of 1/4 inch. The oil should be very hot but don't let it smoke.

Use a large tablespoon to scoop round or pancakes about 3 inches in diameter. Flatten them with the back of the spoon, fry until browned and crispy on both sides. For a deep fryer, mold to similar dimensions by hand. Try to turn only once.

Drain on paper towels, and fry until all the mix is used. Ideally, latkes should be served as soon as possible, but they can be reheated in a 400-degree oven for about 10 minutes; however, they will not be as crispy.

Experiment with dipping the latkes in sour cream, apple sauce, or both.

REFERENCES

Adler, C. (ED.). (1906). *Jewish encyclopedia.* http://www.jewishencyclopedia.com

Appel, G. (2016). *Concise code of Jewish law: A guide to the observance of Shabbat.* D. Goldstein, ED. New York: Maggid.

Appel, G. (1977). *Concise code of Jewish law: compiled from Kitzur Shulhan Aruch and traditional sources.* Ktav Publishing House: New York.

Birnbaum, P. (1979). *Encyclopedia of Jewish concepts.* Hebrew Publishing Company: USA.

Goldstein, Rabbi Z. (1996-2007). *The Complete Friday evening synagogue companion.* The Jewish Learning Group.

Glustrom, S. (1988). *The language of Judaism.* Jason Aronson: New Jersey.

Klagsbrun, F. (1996). *Jewish days: a book of Jewish life and culture around the year.* Harper Collins: USA.

Scherman, Rabbi N. (ED). (1996). *The Artscroll siddur.* Mesorah Publications, Ltd: Brooklyn, NY.

Silberman, S. (1987). *A family Haggadah: In every generation.* Rockville, MD: Kar-Ben Publishing.

Strassfeld, M. (1985). *The Jewish holidays.* New York: Harper & Row Publishers.

INDEX

ABOUT THE AUTHOR

Rabbi S. Creeger's formal education includes an associate degree in nursing from Prince George's Community College; a certificate in Messianic Studies, bachelor's and master's degrees from Messianic Bureau International Yeshiva (MBI); and a Bachelor of Jewish Studies from Baltimore Hebrew University. She was ordained as a Messianic minister in 2000 and then rabbi in 2002 through MBI. Rabbi Creeger served MBI as a teacher, in the office of vice president, and as a member of the advisory board.

Rabbi Creeger has been active in several fields of ministry, serving as counselor and prayer minister in various jails, detention centers, and prisons in the Balt-Wash metro area and to returning veterans from Iraq and Afghanistan in VA hospitals (including Walter Reed) and VFW sites. She has also served as hospital chaplain in Cecil County, Maryland. She and her husband Boaz founded Messianic congregation Beit HaTorah in 1997, and they now maintain a Messianic presence in India and Africa, providing for congregational leaders and the people under their care with educational and training materials and providing financial support for food, clothing, shelter, and medical expenses. These outreaches include orphan care, including the Hadassah Orphanage in India.

Rabbi Creeger may be contacted through her website: www.beithatorah.org

Made in the USA
Middletown, DE
22 September 2018